SAFE @ HOME

SEVEN KEYS TO HOME OFFICE SECURITY

SAFE @ HOME

SEVEN KEYS TO HOME OFFICE SECURITY

BY
JEFFERY D. ZBAR

THE U.S. SMALL BUSINESS ADMINISTRATION'S
2001 SMALL BUSINESS JOURNALIST OF THE YEAR

FirstPublish, Inc.
Orlando, Florida

Safe@Home: Seven Keys to Home Office Security
Copyright ©2001 by Jeffery D. Zbar, Inc. All rights reserved.

Printed in the United States of America. No part of this book may be reproduced or transmitted in any form or by any means, electronic or mechanical, including photocopying, recording, or by any information storage and/or retrieval system, without written permission from the author and publisher. For information, contact Goin' SOHO! Books, a division of Goin' SOHO!, P.O. Box 8263, Coral Springs, Fla., 33075-8263.

ISBN
1-929925-71-9

Library of Congress Cataloging in Publication Data
2001090792

Jeffery D. Zbar
Safe@Home: Seven Keys to Home Office Security

FIRSTPUBLISH, INC.
170 Sunport Ln. Suite 900
Orlando, FL 32809
407-240-1414
www.firstpublish.com

This book, and all my work and success, are dedicated to and a result of my wife, Robbie, and our children, Nicole, Zachary & Zoe. It is only through their acceptance and support of my chosen work style that I have been able to find success in – and sing the praises about – the work-at-home environment. Ah-ooo!

ACKNOWLEDGMENTS

How do you recognize and acknowledge all those individuals whose support and understanding have helped you along your path to success? I guess you start from the beginning.

I thank: my family, who instilled in me the desire for success and the enlightened spark of the entrepreneur from the very beginning; Mrs. Hurley, my 12th Grade English teacher, who introduced me to Expository Writing – which I immediately dreaded but grew to love, and which ultimately led me to where I am today; my editors along the way, who provided outlets for my articles and voice – especially those editors whose publications or Web sites target the same small business, home office and teleworking communities I continue to serve today; and all those allies who provided their ideas, reviewed this manuscript, added bits of wisdom of their own, and generally broadened my viewpoint beyond that little 10-by-14-foot piece of suburbia I call the home office to include the real-life episodes and experiences of today's at-home entrepreneurs and teleworkers.

Most of all, I thank dedicated home officers everywhere, whose growing presence on the American landscape only validates what I knew when I started this work style in the 1980s and increasingly believed along the way: That this is a really cool way to work.

TABLE OF CONTENTS

Introduction 1

CHAPTER I
HOME OFFICE SECURITY:
AN OVERVIEW & A PLAN 10
   Safety & Vulnerability Audit 11
   Security Action Plan & Safety Audit 19

CHAPTER II
HOME OFFICE SECURITY:
THE PREMISES 23
   From the Outside In 23
   Foliage & Lighting 25
   Fences & Gates 30
   Doors, Deadbolts & Locks 31
   Peepholes & Hidden Cameras 36
   Window Security 38
   Alarm Systems 41

CHAPTER III
SECURING THE HOME OFFICE INSIDE 49
   Inventory Your Possessions 50
   Safes & Locking Storage Devices 52
   Childproofing Your Home Office 55
   Personal & Deskside Safety Supplies 57
   Natural Disaster Preparation &
   Action Plan & Contact List 60

CHAPTER IV
HABITS TO IMPROVE SAFETY
& SECURITY 71
   Never Let 'Em See You Working 72
   Preventing Home Invasion 75
   Working with Strangers 77

Thwarting Fraud, Identity Theft
& Client Confidentiality 79
Avoiding Corporate Espionage 83
Insuring the Space 87
Covering the Computer 99

CHAPTER V
COMPUTER, LAPTOP & DATA
SECURITY & PROTECTION 94
Battery Backup and Surge Protection 95
Anti-Virus Protection 97
Firewalls & Anti-Hacking Protection 100
Data Backups 107

CHAPTER VI
PROTECTING YOURSELF OUTSIDE
THE HOME OFFICE 112
Protecting Yourself on the Road 112
Preparing for Travel 114
Protecting Your Laptop 118

CHAPTER VII
WORKSPACE SAFETY & OSHA ISSUES 124
OSHA Issues 124
Survey Your Space for OSHA Violations 125
Ergonomics Blend Mind & Body
in Workplace Function 127
Stress Management 131

APPENDIX 137
The Home Officer's Safety
& Security Checklist 138
SOHO Snapshots: Jane Scheid, Michael Dziak,
Carmen Hiers, Linda Greck & April Spring 140
Index 148
About the Author 150

INTRODUCTION

Is your home as secure as Fort Knox? If you call your home your office, maybe it should be.

From lighting and foliage outside, to window shades, strong deadbolts on the doors and even a flashlight, fire extinguisher or can of Mace® beside your computer, protecting your home, property – and yourself – from any possible emergency, confrontation or intrusion often isn't front-of-mind for the home-based worker. Home officers, including at-home entrepreneurs and teleworkers, are often too concerned with doing the work and delivering the product to consider any potential vulnerability.

Today, more than 12 million Americans run full-time home-based businesses. Another 15 million run businesses after hours from home. Some 23 million Americans telework at least one day a week, and that number is predicted to hit 40 million by 2004, according to research firm Cahners In-Stat. Powering these businesses and home offices are billions of dollars in technology – which handle hundreds of billions of dollars in proprietary, confidential or otherwise sensitive information. Can you afford to lose any of that to accident, theft or natural disaster?

The topic even is relevant for the millions of people who have home offices for no other task than to handle the family finances. The checkbook, credit card and bank statements, investment documents and other sensitive paperwork often are strewn about or filed with little regard for the potential havoc their loss or theft could cause.

Let's face it: Few people like thinking about the bad things that can befall them. But "workplace violence" doesn't begin and end at the corporate office downtown, and even the home office that is little more than a corner desk needs protection. Think about the opportunities you present to the common thief or burglar: You often work in solitude amid expensive and enticing computer and electronic technology – as well as the rest of your home's valuables. You work long hours – possibly with windows or shades open – so outsiders can see you and your belongings. You probably leave the home frequently to get the newspaper, check the mail, take an energizing stroll, or leave for a meeting or the corporate office. Is your shop locked up each time you leave? Do you even pause to consider how safety and security are – or aren't – a part of your daily routine?

Office safety was never the concern of the average office worker; it was always someone else's job. When it comes to a safe and secure workplace, corporate office dwellers benefit from a staff and vendors who oversee everything from security to workplace safety compliance to even the insurance coverage that protects people and tools.

Home officers have no such luxury, and that has to change. Surrounded by technology and other enticements, working with new clients with unknown intentions, or plying the late hours they're known for working – with the telling glow of technology that could attract unsavory characters – you are vulnerable.

Unless you take precautions.

Aside from being the company's president, product manager and back-office worker, you now have to become its *Chief Security Officer*. Thus, along with all the other responsibilities of running your company, you have to make sure your workspace, property – and yourself – all are protected from theft, invasion, burglary or workplace accident or injury.

This is no small responsibility. But it is one of the most overlooked tasks of any home-based worker. Although it's no Fort Knox, your home office can be a bastion of safety and security when you're

INTRODUCTION

working alone. Securing a home office doesn't need to be difficult or challenging. It just has to challenge would-be robbers – and provide the homeowner peace of mind.

Two effective principles are important in the way you protect your home and home office. They help you strengthen your defenses in direct relation to how you perceive your home to look from a criminal's perspective. They're called: Playing the Bad Guy and Layering your Defenses.

- Playing the Bad Guy. How would a burglar look at your home? Would he see doors and windows that are easy to open, plenty of hiding spaces, and a property that is generally "vulnerable"? Or would he see a home where the owner has given thought to eliminating any opportunity for invasion? By surveying your property and looking for the security elements outlined in SOHO Security, you'll understand how a thief views a target – and how to take yours off his list of prospects.
- Layering Your Defenses. This practice requires taking different protective and security features and *layering* them atop one another. For example, after installing proper exterior lighting and foliage to deter prowlers and criminals, have you installed deadbolts and peepholes into the home's solid doors, and are the home's doors and windows are protected by added locks and an alarm system. The worker keeps a flashlight and a cellular phone close at hand when working, and all important information is kept in an office safe or locking drawer or file cabinet. Even the office door has a locking mechanism. Layering creates a *blanket of protection* that helps the home-based worker thwart would-be burglars, and improve your peace of mind.

In this book, you'll learn which safety protocols might be best for your situation, and how to devise a *Security Action Plan* outlining your security measures and updates. This way, you'll know that your home office and business practices are as safe as they can be – and when you need to update that plan as needs change or technology improves.

> # WHAT IF...?
>
> Remember how to play "What if ..."?
>
> As teens learning to drive, many of us were taught to play "What if ...?" What if a car blew through this stop sign, or what if the truck in front of me stopped suddenly, or what if a child ran out into the street? How would we react to the immediacy of the situation, and avoid an accident?
>
> It's a simple game, but one with dramatic implications. And it's a game that has its place in the world of home office safety and security.
>
> What if an intruder confronts you at your front door as you're arriving home? What if a "repairman" comes to the door and requests entry to check a gas leak or electrical problem? What if someone suspicious enters an elevator with you? What if a hurricane approaches, your child gets hold of your files, or your roommate's friend snoops through confidential client documents?
>
> Are you prepared for these scenarios? Reading through this book, you should be envisioning each possible vulnerability you face – the "What If ..." – and then envision a plan of escape or remedy. Your answers should be part of your Security Action Plan, and be ready for implementation if needed. Implementation or remedy could mean carrying Mace ® (where such a product is legal), or installing a home alarm system panic button or knowing your "ambush" code.
>
> Throughout this book, you'll find situations that invite you to play "What If ..." It's an important exercise.

INTRODUCTION

Most important, by reading this book, you should be working from a position of research, planning and thoughtful implementation – rather than by the seat of your pants. To the security professional, that's the most important role of a safe and secure business – even if it's in the home.

"Common sense is the biggest safety feature," says Gil Neuman, chief executive officer of Kent Security Consulting Inc., a North Miami, Fla., security consultancy and alarm service firm. "When people do things out of fear, your common sense doesn't work."

This book is designed to help first-time and veteran at-home workers – and even homeowners and renters – create a safe and secure working and living environment. It applies to anyone who's working from home or from the road.

The book is divided into seven chapters – the *Seven Keys* to creating a safer home office environment – each of which addresses an important element related to safeguarding your home-based workplace. We'll look at securing the home office and its contents from burglary and theft, protecting important files and documents from fires or natural disasters, making your home office more safe for visitors, and even making your workspace ergonomic and OSHA compliant.

Your Seven Keys are:

1. Chapter I. Home Office Security: An Overview and a Plan. This will look at how to survey your property, home and home office – and any existing security elements. You'll learn to gauge your existing vulnerabilities, and then use the rest of the book to strengthen your defenses.

2. Chapter II. Home Office Security: The Premises. Starting from the city street that passes your property, and working your way through any gate, the yard and the front door, you'll consider the security elements that keep bur-

glars and prowlers at bay beyond the confines of the inner sanctum of your home office.

3. Chapter III. Securing the Home Office Inside. Here, you'll look at how to protect your belongings – including your computer, data, files and other sensitive property, whether they're backup diskettes, your business books or paper files. Topics include protection from burglars, roommates, guests and even children – or their visiting friends. Finally, the chapter will discuss how to protect the home office from natural disaster.

4. Chapter IV. Habits to Improve Safety & Security. You've installed the right hardware; here's the mental software you'll need to work safely from home. These practices will be key elements in helping maintain a low profile – from those around you as well as competitors who may seek to steal data.

5. Chapter V. Computer, Laptop & Data Security & Protection. Are your computer and its contents protected? Key issues will include battery back-up and anti-surge devices, anti-virus and anti-hacking protection; and how – and why – to back up sensitive or important data.

6. Chapter VI. Protecting Yourself Outside the Home Office. Are you as safe outside the home office as you are within it? This chapter will discuss protective measures to take while on the road, and how to prepare for travel. You'll also learn how to keep your laptop out of harm's way while traveling.

7. Chapter VII. Workplace Safety & OSHA Issues. Is your home office a safe workplace? Here, you'll see how to ensure your workspace is designed to meet your body's

INTRODUCTION

unique ergonomic needs to ensure physical comfort, productivity and avoidance of any debilitating repetitive stress injuries. Finally, you'll get a primer on how to maintain a positive mental outlook when working from home.

THE TELEWORKER'S PERSPECTIVE

Safe@Home also should be viewed as an essential reference tool to managers or employers with teleworkers. This emerging category of employee spends several days each week or month working from home. He or she often is subjected to the same situations and concerns that the home office entrepreneur would face – whether they be safety, dealing with strangers, maintaining client document confidentiality, ergonomics, or even computer-related safety or performance issues. How well they address safety and security issues can help your company or organization better achieve its goals.

Some of these issues might be news to you – whether you're a home-based entrepreneur, a teleworker or an employer with an at-home work force. After all, how many have thought about security in the home office, or how many have considered the opinion of the Occupational Safety & Health Administration when designing a home-based work space? Although most federal laws affecting the workplace don't apply to home offices, they remain common sense considerations for the savvy home officer.

Home office workers long have been lauded for being an extra set of eyes and ears in the community when the neighbors are commuting and working during the day. We pride ourselves on being able to stand sentry during the work week, when neighborhoods are still and many thieves otherwise would find happy hunting grounds amid quiet residences. Now we must look within – to the need to further protect our own homes from intrusion and invasion.

So read though these pages and consider how to strengthen your security measures so you can run a safe and secure home office.

NOTES:

INTRODUCTION

NOTES:

CHAPTER I
HOME OFFICE SECURITY: AN OVERVIEW & PLAN

Chapter Overview: Corporate America takes its security seriously. So should at-home workers. This chapter will discuss important survey, audit and planning procedures to ensure that your home office has the protective measures it needs to limit a variety of threats.

What does your home office security plan entail? A $99 alarm system without monitoring, a knob lock on the front door – and fingers crossed that no one will ever break in and snatch the computer and other tools that enable you to work and make a living?

We attempt to convince those around us that running a home business is a serious enterprise. So why minimize the importance of our home – and home office – security? Starting from the outside of the average home and working inward, you must look for safety vulnerabilities – and how we can buttress our home offices against intrusion. From the property to the home to the home office – and even how you conduct and protect yourself outside the home office, you'll discover safety and insurance measures designed to keep our work spaces, lives and business enterprises safe, secure and operational amid crisis.

From thorny plants to alarm systems with handheld panic or duress buttons, to fire extinguishers for the home and home office, and even a fireproof safe and file cabinet for safely storing documents and backup data files, protecting and securing the home

HOME OFFICE SECURITY: AN OVERVIEW & A PLAN

office can be an all-encompassing undertaking. It's easy to overlook certain areas of concern.

Daunting and overwhelming? Maybe. The good news is, securing your home office can be a constant work-in-progress, where you add new elements or protective measures as your needs or product offerings change. You may be able to afford a better alarm system with improved features as your business becomes more successful – and you realize a greater need for such security measures.

Some of the personal safety and security tools mentioned in this book, such as an alarm system or the ownership and use of Mace® or pepper spray, might require certification, municipal authorization or some other registration.

CONDUCT A *SAFETY & VULNERABILITY AUDIT* FOR PROTECTION

Have you ever audited your home office? You probably survey your computer hardware to ensure you have the latest equipment – or at least the best to suit your needs. You might even photograph your equipment and write down the serial numbers for safekeeping. But have you ever conducted a *Safety & Vulnerability Audit* to ensure your home is safe from intrusion – from the inside and out?

By conducting the Safety & Vulnerability Audit, you can then use the findings to create a *Security Action Plan*. This document will guide you in the steps necessary to protect – and maintain the security of – your home, home office, contents, computer system – and yourself.

To conduct your Safety & Vulnerability Audit, get a pad of paper and a pen. You will use this to log your findings. Starting from the sidewalk or curb, walk around your property and view it as a passerby or potential burglar would. Do you see ground-level windows with unimpeded access? Tree limbs hanging over the home? No lighting to dissuade criminals from approaching under the cloak of darkness? In fact, survey your surroundings during the day and night, during peak travel and commuting periods and off-peak

> ## WHAT IF...?
>
> ... your corporate office has a security regimen, and your telecommuting plan doesn't? Will your at-home workers follow the corporate guidelines? Should they? It's important to address the potential security breaches that unwittingly can be opened by teleworkers – including corporate espionage, virus introduction, computer theft, home office security and even ergonomics. Following the guidelines throughout this book, put a Telework Security Policy in writing and demand that they follow it.

times. Get to know your neighborhood and the habits of your neighbors.

Using the Home-Based Workplace Safety & Security Audit Worksheet, check Yes or No to the sample questions. Stay alert to those examples of a safe home and workplace that *aren't* on the list. Only you know your home, property, neighbors or traffic patterns. This activity should help you identify strengths and weaknesses in your own home safety regimen, and buttress your defenses against possible intrusion.

HOME-BASED WORKPLACE SAFETY & SECURITY AUDIT WORKSHEET

Y N Doors – including the home office door – are equipped with deadbolts with newly changed locks.

Y N Windows and sliding glass doors are locked and secured against simple intrusion by a burglar using a screwdriver or crowbar to pry open the access points.

Y N Passersby cannot peer easily inside home office from office windows.

Y N Thorny foliage protects windows and other access points.

Y N Exterior light fixtures illuminate your home and property adequately for you to see around your home at night – and dissuade prowlers from visiting your property.

Y N A first aid kit, fire extinguisher, flashlight and personal audible alarm or anti-attack spray are close to the workstation. A portable and cellular phone also are nearby when you are working at night.

Y N The home office furniture meets suggested guidelines for ergonomics; business equipment is placed for peak ergonomic compliance, and the computer screen, keyboard and workplace are cleaned regularly to reduce dust and allergens.

Y N The home worker habitually engages in home office safety measures, such as dimming computer monitor when not in use, closing shades and locking doors. Shades, blinds or other window treatments are closed after hours to shield the home office's interior from the view of outsiders.

Y N The computer is hidden from view in a tower enclosure, and wires are protected from children and pets by a wire chase.

Y N The computer's Internet connection is protected with a firewall and anti-virus software that has been updated within the past two weeks.

Y N All business and expensive personal belongings are inventoried regularly, in case of fire or theft. The list of items and serial numbers, as well as photographs and videotape of the items – and any supporting documents, all are stored off-site.

Y N A 'must call' list of clients and business associates, and peers and managers back at the corporate office (if you're a teleworker), has been created, and a *Home Office Natural Disaster Action Plan* has been written in case a storm or other act of God affects your area.

Y N Travel safety precautions are taken before leaving on a business or pleasure trip, including preparing the home office for vacancy, and gathering the appropriate tools to protect yourself and your laptop (if appropriate) while on the road.

Audit Worksheet Scoring Key: While the goal would be to have as many "yes" answers as possible, no combination or compilation of scores is better or worse when grading this worksheet. With each question, you should be envisioning how each element improves upon the layering effect, ultimately to improve your home office security regimen. If you see a pattern of vulnerabilities – for example, the outside has no lighting or foliage to thwart burglars, and the home's locks are aged and weak – it may be time to revisit those areas of your home's protection.

HOME OFFICE SECURITY: AN OVERVIEW & A PLAN 15

Image ©2000 John Hancock

Important Security Elements

1. Window treatments. Closing window shades in the home office prevents outsiders from being able to peer inside the workspace, especially when you're not in the office. Close the shades when working at night, since it's more difficult to see out than in when it's dark outside. Shades also help deflect heat and keep the space cooler in the summer.

2. Dim the screen. Turn off or down the monitor when you're not working. A monitor's glow can attract the attention of outsiders and alert them to the presence of a computer and other expensive equipment.

3. Desk-top safety devices. Desk-top safety devices should include a powerful flashlight in case the power goes out at night; a personal audible alarm in case of threat by a prowler or intruder; a can of Mace ® or other personal

defense spray; a fire extinguisher; a first aid kit; a cellular phone, in case the phone lines are cut or phone service goes down; and a remote control panic button for the home's alarm system.

4. Window locks. Keyed or toggle window locks, or a strip of wood placed or secured in the window track, can prevent the window from being opened from the outside.

5. Deadbolts. Installing a locking device in the office door can prevent entry by kids, roommates, guests and others – especially if you're not home and someone breaks in.

6. Alarm systems. A home alarm system can protect the home and home office. Request that each window and door entry have contacts installed, and that glass breakage detectors, motion detectors, and heat and smoke detectors are installed to protect the entire home from a variety of threats. Purchase a remote control panic button, and learn how to use keypad functions like Ambush, Instant and other emergency codes. Alarms may result in lower insurance premiums. A sign on the front yard can alert passersby to the presence of the alarm system.

7. Exterior lights. Installing lights with motion detectors on the corners of the home can illuminate the property and dissuade prowlers.

8. Thorny plants. Planting thorny plants outside windows around the home can thwart burglars' attempts at entry. As they thicken, the plants will further impede the view inside while not preventing you from seeing out. They also can beauty and value to the home. Beware allowing thick hedges or shrubs from creating hiding places for prowlers.

HOME OFFICE SECURITY: AN OVERVIEW & A PLAN

9. Protect visitors, Part I. Is the approach to your home safe? Fix or replace broken stepping stones, wobbly steps to the home, and put children's toys or other obstacles away before clients, customers or business guests arrive. A trip and fall could be a liability nightmare, and a more presentable home offices leaves a better impression on your visitors.

10. Protect visitors, Part II. Large or aggressive dogs should be kept in a room or in the yard before guests arrive. Also, ask you insurance agent about additional liability or personal injury coverage for the home and home office to protect you against claims in case of injury.

THE SECURITY ACTION PLAN

If some emergency were to affect you or your home office, do you know how you would react? Now is the time to play *Chief Security Officer* and devise a plan that can help you see your way to safety in the event of almost *any* foreseeable emergency. This can include a burglary or home invasion, thwarting corporate espionage, working with a stranger, diminishing the effects of a natural disaster, or even protecting yourself and your equipment while traveling.

Your *Security Action Plan* should cover all these contingencies. Similar to the way you would prepare a business plan or a marketing plan, this written document should take time and thoughtful consideration to research and write.

Written elements of your *Security Action Plan* should include (at a minimum):

- An assessment of critical safety and security areas and protocols.
- Data backup regimen, timetables and follow through.
  Emergency escape exits and meeting plans for family or other residents.

- Emergency shutdown and removal functions and equipment.
- Natural Disaster Planning, including names and numbers of important emergency contacts. You cannot rely on memory to piece together a hurried list of essential contacts if you are evacuating the office because of a natural disaster.
- Family contingencies. For parents who work from home, family often comes first. Any Emergency Action Plan should place the family high on the list. If children are in the home, include in the plan a discussion of how they are to get out of the home in an emergency, and where the family should meet if everyone gets separated or leaves through different exits. A fixed object, such as a curbside mailbox or tree, usually is a good location.

Once the plan is completed, print it out, and revisit it frequently. It must become an important part of your business operations. Only if you treat your *Security Action Plan* as a serious element of your business will it help to protect and secure your home business or home office adequately for the long term.

HOME OFFICE SECURITY: AN OVERVIEW & A PLAN

THE HOME OFFICE SECURITY ACTION PLAN

This Security Action Plan was developed on (insert date) to achieve maximum effective safety and security and limit the vulnerabilities of my home and home office.

1. The property owner or renter conducted a safety audit and determined the home's weaknesses and areas that need further protection. The surrounding property, the home's exterior, access points, and its view from the street, sidewalk or other thoroughfares were surveyed. Vulnerabilities were noted (as suggested in the Home-Based Workplace Safety & Security Audit Worksheet, and actions and interventions needed were implemented.
2. Implementation of the security regimen was completed. Areas identified and addressed include:
    a. Outdoor lighting was added and foliage planted as needed to illuminate the property and eliminate access to window.
    b. Access points, including *all* entry doors, windows and sliding glass doors, were examined, and new deadbolt or window locks were installed where appropriate.
    c. The need for a residential alarm system was considered.
3. The residential insurance agent was contacted to discuss the need for additional insurance coverage for the home-business use of computers and other technology. Where appropriate, additional insurance coverage was purchased.
4. A computer data backup regimen is executed in which critical files are backed up daily or weekly, and an entire hard drive data backup is conducted monthly. The backup media are stored off-site to prevent damage or theft.
5. Anti-virus software and a computer firewall were installed and are activated to run in the background to provide protection against viruses, corruption and hacking. The anti-

virus software is updated weekly. If the equipment is owned by the employer of a teleworker, appropriate anti-virus and firewall measures were undertaken by the corporate Information Technology department, or authorization was issued for the teleworker to conduct such installations.

6. When necessary, the home office's entry door is locked when the worker is not on premises. Confidential client paperwork is stored in a locking file cabinet, and sensitive or financial home-business and personal documents are kept in a locking desk drawer or other safe location. If necessary, the computer tower is housed in a closing and/or locking enclosure to protect it from intrusion or tampering by family or intruders.

7. The *Home Office Natural Disaster Action Plan* (see Chapter III) includes a full protocol of actions in the event of a pending natural disaster or the possibility of an act of God.

8. In case of fire, essential data have been duplicated and stored off-site. A backup diskette for recent data has been created and placed in an accessible location in the event of a fast exit.

9. If appropriate, this program has been reviewed with corporate telemanagers and security officers to ensure it meets or exceeds the company's standards for safety and security, ergonomics and liability issues.

10. Every three months beginning on (_____), the home officer reviews the *Home-Based Workplace Safety & Security Audit Worksheet* to ensure the home's vulnerabilities are limited. If other family members or residents live on site, every three months home office security is discussed to ensure continued safety is maintained.

Date Last Reviewed: _____

Reviewed By: _____

NOTES:

NOTES:

CHAPTER II
HOME OFFICE SECURITY: THE PREMISES

Chapter Overview: A safe home office starts from the outside and works its way in. From lush and thorny plants outside windows to dissuade a break-in, to windows and doors that lock securely, to alarm systems designed to provide vault-like protection from break-in, this chapter will address how your premises should demonstrate a serious consideration about security.

FROM THE OUTSIDE IN

What do passersby or burglars see from the street or sidewalk outside? Can they clearly see an array of expensive technology perched an arm's reach inside your home office window? Do they see a computer screen glowing at night, with no outdoor lighting to dissuade their access to your home? Can they walk right up to your home office window – under the cloak of darkness– and jimmy your window open with a simple screwdriver or pocket knife?

Can they make off with the tools of your livelihood without your or your neighbors' knowing – leaving you stripped of your business information, archives and your peace of mind in the process?

Or do they see a home office fortified against potential intrusion? Do they see plants by the windows – which block their view inside? Do they see shades drawn shut at night, so intruders have no idea what is going on inside the home – or that there even is a home office inside? Do they see a home security company alarm sign in your yard or stickers in your windows to tell them security is an important concern for this residence?

In other words, do they sense an open invitation to prey on the weak, or will they pass by your home in search of another, less protected residence? Which image would you rather project?

THE HOME PROTECTION SURVEY

Because home – and home office – security starts outside, and works its way in from there, you must too. You can't know how criminals view your home unless you see it from their perspective. To do so, grab a pad and pen and step outside. Take a walk around your home and property. Even if you live in an apartment complex, your doorways and windows need to be surveyed and secured against theft or unlawful entry. If you find weaknesses, report them – in writing – to your landlord.

Survey your structure from all sides – the street or sidewalk out front, the alley in back, even from the neighbors' properties. Do entry points or hiding places aid in a home invasion or burglary?

When surveying the home and home office for areas in need of protection, look for these telltale signs:

- Is the property open and clear? Or is it surrounded by thick or overgrown foliage that provides hiding places for prowlers?
- Is it well-lighted at night to dissuade prowlers? Lighting should include not only the front alcove but also the perimeter and property.
- Is each entry point wired into the home's alarm system, as opposed to just the front and rear doors?
- Are fence gates locked with padlocks to deter entry – and make carrying out large items difficult?

HOME OFFICE SECURITY: THE PREMISES

FROM THE CURB TO THE OUTSIDE WALLS

FOLIAGE & OUTDOOR LIGHTING

Some of the most easily overlooked elements of home office security are those features that can add attractiveness and value to your home: foliage and outdoor lighting. Plants can impede passersby's view of your home's interior, while not inhibiting your view of the world outside. Permanent lighting, whether automatic or on a sensor or timer, can bathe your home's exterior and the surrounding property in attractive light that also can thwart a burglar's or prowler's advances. In this section, we'll look at how these ornamental elements can add to both the home's aesthetics and security.

GO GREEN

Plant thorny bushes or thick hedges outside every window of the home, especially outside the home office. With many plants, as they grow, their briars will thicken, diminishing access to your home's entry points and outsiders' view in. This still will provide those inside with a clear view outside. Prickly plants also will impede the intrusion of nuisance animals.

Here's a sample list of common thorny plants:

- Spanish bayonets
- Cactus
- Century plants
- Bougainvillea
- Blackberry shrubs and vines
- Pyracantha (the fire thorn bush)
- Dragon lady and rotunda holly
- Argentine mesquite
- Catclaw acacia
- Prickly pears

- Rose bushes
- Large, subtropical ornamental palms include roebellini, sago and Aiphane.

Plants vary by climate or region. Check with your local nursery, horticulturalist or home-improvement garden center to see which species match your geography.

Look for these beneficial elements related to foliage:

- Buy plants that grow tall and thick enough to both impede view as well as prevent prowlers from gaining access to your home office.
- Look for plants that will not disturb your view outside while seated in your home office or any room with a window at or near eye level; in many instances, you will be able to see passersby without their seeing you.
- The right foliage will shade the office from direct sunlight during morning or afternoon, when the sun's angle can shine rays directly into the office, heating the space and making work uncomfortable.
- When choosing your plants and their placement, be wary of creating hiding places for prowlers.

Whenever possible, keep the foliage near the home's entrance attractive but appropriately thin. The walkway or approach to your home is not the best place for heavy, thick or tall foliage. This can provide prowlers an opportunity to hide from view and ambush you, another resident, your employees or guests. Thick foliage also encourages standing water or high moisture, which could aid in the breeding of mosquitoes, the nesting of rats or birds, and the harboring of other pests.

Thinning out foliage should include clipping or pruning large tree branches or limbs that extend to, touch or overhang the home, awning, roof or windows. These can provide access to the roof, eaves, awnings and the home or its entry points. They also can give prowlers a perch from which to survey your home – or hide until you enter or exit the property. Keeping trees thinned of excess foliage and branches can add additional light beneath the canopy during the day, and deter criminals as well as nuisance animals.

LIGHTIN' UP

Landscape lighting can help keep a home's perimeter, property and structure well-lighted to discourage unwelcome guests. Lighting the home and premises serves multiple purposes for the home business owner – and homeowner. Use of accent and landscape lighting can beautify the property, and bathe the yard in light. Done well, the lighting also can dissuade prowlers from selecting the residence for attack. This doesn't mean you need to wash your property in light, and make it look like a car dealership with excessive wattage. Lighting can be subtle and attractive – and quite effective.

Start near the home. Each point of entry should be well-lighted with fixtures situated above or beside the doorway. The corners of the structure should have flood lamps mounted downward from the soffit and pointing perpendicularly from each other down different sides of the structure. Mounting the lighting from the soffit, or underside of the roof's overhang that on most homes extends beyond the vertical exterior walls, places it too high for most people to reach without the aid of a stepladder or other platform.

Flood lamps will illuminate large swaths of property or foliage, where accent lighting will provide softer light – while still providing the desired illumination to thwart unwanted visitors and pests. Low-voltage lights can brighten walkways and driveways and help neighbors to see and report suspicious activities.

Make sure that any lights that illuminate the home don't shine into the office or other windows, and impair the view outside the home. Check the fixtures' positioning frequently at night to ensure they maintain proper alignment.

To increase the effectiveness and security measure of any outdoor lighting, install a motion detector, light sensor or timer. With many of these devices, if the circuit on which the light is on is controlled by an interior light switch, someone inside can flip the switch off and on quickly to turn on the lights – even if no one has tripped the motion detector or it's not time or dark enough for the timer or light sensor to turn them on. This can help make walking around outside more safe.

Which device – motion detector, light sensor or timer – you use depends on your particular needs:

- Motion detectors: These units detect the movement of people, animals, automobiles and other objects that pass within their range. They turn on the lights, which usually will stay on for a desired period of time – from seconds to minutes. Motion detectors typically employ passive infrared receivers (PIR) or photoelectric beams to sense motion. Passive infrared receiver units detect infrared frequency radiation emitted by the human body; older units may detect heat emissions from passing animals. But because these devices are more sensitive than traditional motion detectors, they therefore can reduce false activation from swaying trees, leaves, branches, limbs or other such objects. Photoelectric beam motion detectors emit a narrow light beam from a transmitter to a receiver; some use reflectors to complete the transmission. They commonly are used as security features for alarms, and even are used to illuminate areas that are frequented by rodents or other pests. Any object, person or animal that crosses the beam engages the unit. The light is switched on, and in some models a sound or other audible alarm is engaged to scare away pests or intruders. The lights might become bothersome to you – and your neighbors – if your street has a lot of foot or vehicular traffic. In that case, decrease the detector's sensitivity by increasing the range of the sensor (usu-

HOME OFFICE SECURITY: THE PREMISES

ally accomplished with a screwdriver or by hand). You can adjust this frequently as your needs or conditions change.

- Small area motion detectors: Sometimes, having more protection around certain windows or doorways of the home will decrease your vulnerability to invasion – and boost your peace of mind. Motion detectors with audible alarms can be installed easily outside your home office window or doorway, or any easily accessible first floor window. Usually used to keep outdoor animals out of garbage bins, these detectors emit a loud noise and pulsating light when the infrared beam is broken. A timer can be used to adjust the duration of the alarm. Most models operate on batteries or AC adapters.
- Single outlet motion sensors: These switches screw into an existing standard light bulb socket, turning it into an effective motion-sensing light fixture. Simply remove the existing bulb and screw in the light sensor. As with most sensors, you can adjust the time that the light stays on. One downside: If the light socket is within a larger housing or fixture, adding the sensor could make the bulb and sensor too long for the existing fixture. In this case, you can opt for a shorter bulb, although you likely will lose wattage and brightness.
- Light sensors: These units turn on the lights as the outside natural light fades. They are ideal for areas that must be illuminated at all nighttime hours, such as parking lots, or high-traffic pedestrian areas. When attached to an interior light switch, they can be turned off or on as needed.
- Timers: As do light sensors, timers engage lights for a longer duration. In this case, the user would preset the time desired for the light to be on, for example, from sunset to midnight. As with other types of light control devices, they often can be overridden by an interior switch. And in latitudes where days grow longer or shorter with the progres-

sion of the calendar or where daylight savings is observed, they will have to be adjusted accordingly.

The best and safest way to install the wiring to power your exterior lighting is to install high-quality "Romex" or insulated, industrial electrical cable through the attic or walls, if possible. This highly insulated wire is less prone to deterioration due to exposure to the elements, or and it is less likely to cause a fire hazard. Running the cable through the attic will hide the wiring and protect it from a prowler or burglar's wire cutters. With any outdoor lighting, make certain all exposed electrical cable is housed or sheathed in plastic or metal conduit. This will prevent or dissuade criminals from cutting or tampering with the wire. It also will keep code inspectors from citing you for having exposed cabling – which in many jurisdictions will not meet the building code. Call an electrician to handle any installations that may be unsafe or beyond your experience or capabilities.

FENCES & GATES

Many homeowners like fences for the positive feeling they provide. A good fence can demarcate property lines and "make good neighbors," as Robert Frost so concisely noted. A fence with a closed and locked gate can keep kids and pets in, and keep other kids from ambling onto your property. Fences also can keep others out, particularly large rodents, dogs and other animals. A fence can help deter thieves by creating a physical and psychological barrier to entry. Fences with narrow and locked gates can prevent burglars from both entering your property, as well as from easily carrying away such large items as television sets, computers and monitors.

What else can you do to improve your fence's ability to deter outsiders? By attaching a door retractor to gates, you can ensure the entry is closed after each time someone passes through. This will keep animals out, and a closed gate will be less inviting to a prowler or burglar than a gate left open. It also will help keep children and

HOME OFFICE SECURITY: THE PREMISES

pets from roaming free. Along with the closing device, install a gate latch that automatically locks when the gate is pushed shut. This will ensure the wind, a child or a pet doesn't open the gate without your knowledge. As an added security measure, install a lock on every gated entrance. Using either a key or combination lock, you can ensure your gates stay closed.

What about a living fence? A hedge planted along the perimeter of the property – alongside the fence – will beautify the home, while also providing added privacy and security. The hedge will block the view of others from the outside, helping keep prying eyes out. This is an added security measure, especially if expensive home office or home entertainment center equipment is otherwise visible from the outside. Depending on the species, spacing each plant about 18 inches to 24 inches apart along the fence line will help ensure full growth. Coupled with the fence, they will provide added security around the home's property line.

> **WHAT IF...?**
>
> ... you placed a "Beware of Dog" sign on each gate? Even if you don't have a dog, this can be a deterrent to criminals. Check local zoning ordinances on the type and style of sign required in your municipality. Condo or townhome residents who cannot have pets might have to bypass this tip.

DOORS, DEADBOLTS & LOCKS

THE DOORS

Doors often are your first line of defense from intrusion. A strong door with a powerful deadbolt can both beautify and fortify your home and home office against frontal assault. When upgrading your doors or selecting doors for a new home, don't forget that patio doors, those leading out of the garage as well as the front door need to be considered.

When installing a "pre-hung" door that includes the doorframe, consider one with the hinges on the inside. Having the hinges inside the home can help protect the residence from an intruder who otherwise would tap out the hinge pins with a hammer and screwdriver. In northern climates, where doors typically open to the inside, this often isn't a necessary consideration. In warmer climates, on the other hand, hinges often are on the outside. This can present a security breach. Consider installing hasps, which are two-piece couplers that, when combined with the door's deadbolt, will not allow removal of the door – even if exposed, outside hinge pins have been tampered with or removed.

The doorframe is almost as important as the door itself. In fact, the doorway is as vulnerable as the weakest element of the door and doorframe. When installing new frames, look for sturdy wood or steel construction, with the wood no less than two inches thick. If your home has a hollow steel or aluminum frame, protect against the use of a crowbar for entry by filling the gaps and air spaces with cement or tile grout. Inspect your exterior doorways frequently for rot, splitting or other deterioration. With steel and wooden doorframes, consider removing shorter screws anchoring the frame to the home and replacing them with longer lag bolts or screws.

Also consider door hinges that have pin butts. These are screws that lock the pin permanently in position, preventing tampering or removal.

If your home's front entrance has double doors, take added precautions to secure this entry point. After all, the primary door used for entry is only as secure as the door to which it locks. The inactive door should have flush or cane bolts that extend from the frame and threshold at least one inch into the ceiling and floor. When closed and locked, neither door should have any give or wiggle. Allowances will provide burglars a possible space or crack into which to slip a crowbar, long screwdriver, long knife or other lever with which to pry the doors apart or open.

HOME OFFICE SECURITY: THE PREMISES

> ## WHAT IF...?
>
> ... someone tried to break into your home via an exterior door? Are all those doors made of solid wood or steel construction, including the door leading outside to the garage and from the garage to the house? Do they feature deadbolt locks with tumblers that have been changed since the last resident or tenant lived in the home? Also consider a barrier bar. This locking device is anchored the width of the door, and prevents its opening from the outside.

DEADBOLTS

For many, the deadbolt is the first line of defense of the home or home office. Its key often is large and prominent on the key ring, almost exuding an aura of security. But is the deadbolt actually strong enough to secure the home from forced entry?

There are several important features to look for in a deadbolt. The case-hardened steel bolt that actually secures the door should extend at least one inch into the door frame or facing door. By also using a steel or brass strike plate through which the bolt slides into the frame or facing door, you can possibly further secure the home by preventing a burglar from using a crowbar or screwdriver to break or pry away the wood or concrete in which the bolt rests.

The cylinder guard – or primary housing of the lock – should be solid metal, and must be circular, spherical or tapered to prevent grasping by a wrench or pliers. No screwheads should be exposed outside the home, and all connecting screws should always be inside the home.

Styles of deadbolt locks include:

> ## WHAT IF...?
>
> ... a child were playing around your front door, or a lawn or maintenance man were raking the bushes outside your front door and came across a hidden key? Bingo! Instant entry. What's worse, many people hide keys – and forget about them. *Never hide keys outside.* Give duplicates to close neighbors, or nearby family or friends.

- Double-key or double-cylinder deadbolt lock: This style of deadbolt requires a key to open the door from the inside or outside. This unique safety feature ensures that, even if a burglar has broken a glass pane in the door or a window close enough to reach the lock, without the key, he will not be able to retract the bolt. A word of caution, though: Use of this lock can create a safety or fire hazard when the home is occupied. Keep the key required to open the lock nearby inside the house, and make sure all residents know where it is and how to use it.
- Thumb-turn lock or single-cylinder deadbolt. This deadbolt lock is the most common lock on the market. It requires a key to open from the outside but can be opened easily from the inside with a turn of the knob. Again, the greatest vulnerability here is if the home has glass in the door or a window within reach of the knob. By breaking the glass, a burglar easily could gain entry by unlocking the door. Make sure any single-cylinder deadbolt used is at least 40 inches – or an average man's arm length – from a window or other glass pane.
- Keyless, push-button deadbolt. This locking apparatus requires no electronics. Once it is installed, the user simply punches in a multidigit code on a keypad of a half-dozen

HOME OFFICE SECURITY: THE PREMISES

buttons. Once the right code is entered, turn a knob and the door can be opened. Simple to use, the lock's combination can be changed simply as desired.

Other simple locking devices, such as chain latches, key-in-knob locks or dead-latch locks, often are not reliable, stand-alone security devices. Each is fallible and provides limited safety features as compared to the deadbolt. Chain latches can be torn from the door frame with a kick or stiff shove. Key-in-knob locks provide meager security, and their short bolt can be easily picked by a good thief with a simple credit card.

When you move into a new home or apartment, have a locksmith change the locks by re-keying all the tumblers. Although our inclination might be to trust the former resident, you probably don't really know him or her – or all the people to whom they might have given a key. You either can remove the tumbler and take it to a locksmith or home-improvement center, or hire a locksmith to visit your home to do the job. Even if you believe you lost a key, have the lock changed. The expense is well worth the peace of mind that comes with knowing your home is secure.

If you share your residence with roommates, a deadbolt installed on your bedroom or home office door can provide additional security. Although you may trust them, you don't know the intentions of others they may invite into the home. Your materials – and your clients' projects – should be considered valuable and confidential enough to protect this way. Even if you work from home alone or with your immediate family, a deadbolt or lock on the home office door can help keep your materials private, and help prevent any unintentional damage or chaos caused by young children.

How important are your personal, business and client files? Important enough to protect with a lock and key? Either buy a file cabinet with a lock pre-installed, or most cabinets already have a lock hole stamped into the face. To install a lock, punch out the metal tab, and purchase and install the appropriate lock. Contact your nearby office supply superstore or the cabinet manufacturer to

> ## WHAT IF...?
>
> ... you weren't home and a prowler, burglar or even an unseemly houseguest or roommate was already inside your home and standing at your office door? What would keep him or her from entering your workspace and rifling through your files, company checkbook or other confidential items? *Install – and use – a deadbolt on the office door.* This can prevent entry to the workspace, even by roommates or children, when you're not around.

learn which lock fits your cabinet. If you don't think you need to install a lock on every cabinet or desk drawer, choose one on which to install a lock. Each time you leave the office, make sure office valuables – including backup files, the company and personal checkbook and extra checks, and other sensitive client correspondence and documents – are secured in that drawer. Then lock it. Along with a locked office door, a locked home and an alarm system, you can create a layering effect that will further protect your most valuable belongings.

Peepholes & Hidden Cameras

The doorbell rings. You're about to open the door, but you hesitate. "Do I know who it is? Am I presenting an opportunity for invasion?" Smart questions. You need to think of solutions before the situation arises.

Knowing who is at your door can be your best defense against intrusion. You can see whether the visitor is a friend, family member, the usual delivery driver – or a stranger wanting you to open the door for reasons unknown. The more information you can process before you let people in, the safer and better you feel about your

HOME OFFICE SECURITY: THE PREMISES

> ## WHAT IF...?
>
> ... you opened your front door to let a cool breeze blow in? Are you also inviting unwanted visitors? Install a metal-framed screen door with its own deadbolt. This will ensure your space is safe when you leave your door open.

home. Installation and use of a peephole or electronic visual device can help you make an informed decision about who's there, whether he or she poses a possible threat, and how you should deal with the situation.

A peephole can let you see who is outside your front door. This is an especially important device if your doors have no glass within them, and there are no windows nearby to allow you a view outside.

A wide-angle peephole installed in the front door can provide almost 180-degree viewing. This will allow you to see people standing right in front of the door, or anyone who might be trying to avoid your sight by standing off to one side.

High-Tech Viewers

A common high-tech visual aid is a new line of barely visible outdoor surveillance cameras that can be installed anywhere around the home or office's entrance. Used in tandem with an intercom, the video camera's image and audio feed can be linked to any room in the home – including the home office, bedroom or kitchen, and even the computer monitor. Using this device, you can see and hear who is at the door, without having to leave your seat or the room you are in.

Several models can be outfitted with a video or still-image recorder, which can take a digital "snapshot" of the last 60 people who rang the doorbell. Contact an alarm or security system provider to see which models are available for your home.

When traveling or working outside the home, products like HAI Web-Link II (www.homeauto.com) allow homeowners to access remotely via the Internet a home automation system, including video or audio surveillance systems and other key controls. Users also can access other automation-linked services, such as turning on or off the alarm system or interior or exterior lighting. The system also will alert the homeowner via electronic mail if the alarm has been set off.

As with most wired technology for the home, it can be more cost-effective to consider these upgrades during a new home's construction, or when you move into a new residence. During construction when the walls have not yet been erected, wiring work is easier to do than if the technician has to "snake" the wiring down through the attic after construction is completed.

WINDOW SECURITY

The average home could have four or five times as many windows as doors. But, often, homeowners only think of doors as potentially vulnerable points of entry. In reality, how secure are your windows? In many homes, they're a frequently overlooked entry point. Yet, protecting your windows from outside access can be simple and practical.

How to secure your windows depends on which kind of windows you have. The most common types are handle operated awning windows, double-hung windows, casement windows, sliding windows and doors, and old-style jalousie windows which feature separate, long and narrow glass slats – any one of which can be removed from the outside. Even window- or wall-mounted air conditioners, whose installation creates another point of entry into the home, present potential security breaches. Each window offers its own unique security challenges – and solutions.

HOME OFFICE SECURITY: THE PREMISES

Here's a few ways to secure your windows:

- Install locks on your windows and sliding glass doors to prevent their being opened from the outside. The local home center has keyed locks that are installed easily and provide reliable, easy-to-use security and protection. Simple plastic locking mechanisms also can be purchased at the local home improvement center. These affix to the window or sliding glass door to keep it from sliding open. Just be sure to place it out of reach of small children.

  Awning windows, which are opened by turning a handle, may seem tightly closed but can present opportunity to burglars and home invaders. Your preventive safety measures should include: making sure they're tightly closed and removing the handle (done either by slipping the handle off, or loosening a screw in the handle, and then removing the handle).

- Sliding glass doors should be secured with an auxiliary lock or pin. Hire a handyman to drill a hole through the upper corner of a sliding glass door, and only through the first piece of metal in the backing door. You then can slip a large nail into the hole to secure one door to the other; the same works with some kinds of windows, including double-hung windows. If you do it yourself, be sure not to touch the hidden glass with the drill; it will shatter and is expensive to replace.

- Slip a thin piece of wood into the floor track of your sliding glass door to further prevent its being opened. You can do the same in the vertical tracks of a traditional window. Visit your local hardware store to purchase a piece of scrap lumber to suit your needs.

- Jalousie windows, which are found in older homes, present the greatest vulnerability. In homes where the windows no longer open or are never used, affix each slat into its frame with epoxy glue or contact cement. A more secure alternative would be to buy and install a sturdy metal grate with bars close enough to prevent a criminal from slipping his hand through to open the grate or unlock the door (if the jalousies are in or near a door). In fact, increase your security by doing both.

- Professionally installing your window- or wall-mounted air conditioner units can ensure the unit isn't stolen or removed to provide entry to the home. Contract an air conditioner service technician to attach the housing to the machine itself with screws. You also can secure the metal housing to the home with nails, screws or metal hurricane straps. If the home has an alarm system, have the unit wired into the system to prevent theft or removal for entry.
- Storm, basement and garage windows should be reinforced with additional protection against vandalism and break-in.
- Install grates or locks on each window to prevent entry. With any window locking devices, *keep the keys handy* to ensure you can vacate the premises quickly if the front door is blocked in an emergency.
- As with all security precautions, *check frequently* to ensure your locks and devices are still engaged – especially if you have young children in the home.

Window Treatments

Sometimes, the best theft protection is never to let an outsider see what's going on inside the home in the first place. The lure of computers, stereos, televisions, antiques and other expensive belongings are a strong enticement for the criminal element. By shielding your home's interior from their view you can help prevent the enticement – and break-in.

Window treatments, such as curtains, blinds, shades, awnings or even tinting, can block or diminish passersby's view into your home. Used appropriately, they also help reduce sunlight and heat into the office in the early morning or late afternoon. A room-darkening

HOME OFFICE SECURITY: THE PREMISES

pull-down blind can help reduce heat and decrease discoloration of your window treatment fabric. Because they serve both security and aesthetics, choose your window treatment based on both needs.

> **WHAT IF...?**
>
> ... someone threw a brick through your window to gain entry? Prevent this opportunity by installing *window safety film*. The polyester film comes clear, or tinted, which can reduce heat and sunlight into the home. Available at your local home improvement center, it might not prevent breakage. But it is designed to keep the glass intact to prevent flying objects from entering the home.

You either can hire a professional window treatment company to handle the installation or do it yourself. If you elect to install your own window treatments, make sure they fit well. Measure the height and width of the interior window casement; any areas left uncovered when the shades are drawn closed could provide a view in from the outside.

Automatic blinds can be set to open or close at specific times, or by heat, light exposure or other preset adjustments. They can be set to close before the afternoon rush hour, when more people may be walking past your windows. Use of automatic blinds also can help deter burglars while you're away by giving the appearance that someone is in the home adjusting the shades.

ALARM SYSTEMS

If a man's home is his castle, as English common law declared, then his alarm system can be his sentry standing guard when the king is away or at rest. Alarm systems provide a reliable first line of defense for the home and home office, especially when the resident is not at home. No longer an expensive commodity, most are priced right for any consumer. And if you work from home, an alarm can provide added peace of mind knowing that your hardware and confidential client, corporate or personal files are safe.

But how do you select your alarm system? Working with an alarm expert or consulting and installation company, you can determine your requirements based on your specific needs and your residential setting.

WHAT IF...?

... a burglar sees a screen glowing in your office? *Dim your computer screen* – and lower the shades – when you're not in the office, especially at night. A monitor glowing from a home office advertises that the home has a computer and probably other expensive office hardware on the premises. Eliminate the enticement by hiding the equipment from view.

Alarms are available in two configurations: wired and wireless. Wired systems have actual copper wiring that is snaked throughout the home, reaching every window, door and other entry and safety device, to complete the system. Wireless systems use radio frequency transmitters and receivers to complete the system and protect the home.

Shopping your alarm by price? Beware. Although alarm systems are advertised at $99 – plus a monthly monitoring fee of around $25, that most likely will protect one or two doors, few if any windows, and provide only one keypad. The average single-family home might have at least three doors, a dozen or more windows, and possibly several sliding glass doors. Most experts advise protecting every entry into the home, as well as installing internal safety mechanisms to protect the dwelling in case someone were to get past the alarm.

HOME OFFICE SECURITY: THE PREMISES

The cost to protect an entire home runs around $1 a square foot – and higher, depending on the added measures, such as motion detectors, glass-breakage sensors, hot-wired smoke detectors and the like. Monthly monitoring contracts average $25 a month extra.

If the home has no alarm system, a basic system covering several doors and windows can be purchased for less than $100 – plus around $25 a month for monitoring. Providers, such as Brinks, ADT, AmeriTech and SecurityVillage.com, provide such services, although basic alarms lack such important security features as extra keypads for frequently used entrances, contacts on every door and window, and motion, glass breakage and smoke detectors.

WHAT IF...?

... you asked your insurance company whether it offers a reduced premium for an alarm system? You could enjoy a discount of upward of 10 percent or more a year. It often increases based on whether the system includes smoke and detectors, and whether the system is wired to a central monitoring service.

THE ALARM: BASIC FEATURES

With so many providers, how should you know which alarm system to choose? Most come with a variety of basic features and benefits, including:

- Central station monitoring: This is the monitoring service that is alerted when your alarm is tripped. Once notified that the alarm has been set off, the service then call the home owner or other contact to learn whether it was a false alarm. In that case, the homeowner provides a name and secret password. If no one answers, or if whoever answers

the phone cannot provide the password, the police are dispatched to the residence.
- Monitoring of each point of entry. Some advertised alarm company special offers monitor only select doors or windows. Experts advise protecting each point of entry, including all doors and windows.
- Battery backup in the event of power failure. This is a battery installed with the system to ensure the unit stays engaged, even if the home loses power. Check your battery every two years.
- Automatically shut off and reset. If the alarm is set off while you're away, it should turn off and reset itself every 15 minutes or so. This can be adjusted with some models.
- An audible sounding device. The alarm's horn or bell should be loud enough to be heard both by any occupants of the home as well as your neighbors.
- Underwriters Laboratories Inc. (U.L.) approval. This certifies that the system meets established industry standards.

Even if all the windows have magnets to sense when the window has been opened, what if a burglar simply breaks the glass? Magnets can't detect that. Instead, alarm technicians install glass-breakage and acoustic sensors in key locations throughout the home to detect the distinct frequency of broken glass. They also sell window shock sensors, which detect strong impact against a window or sliding glass door. Homes with French, sliding glass or other doors with extensive use of glass need both magnetic contacts that sense opening of the door and broken-glass sensors.

Alarms don't only monitor for break-ins. Using heat and smoke detectors placed throughout the home protects the family, business and property against fire. Alarm experts recommend installation of heat detectors in and around the kitchen, and smoke detectors near the sleeping areas of the home. A smoke detector in or near the home office also would alert you to any fire or smoke while working, or if a fire broke out in your home office.

HOME OFFICE SECURITY: THE PREMISES

As with many electronics on the market today, alarm systems are rife with features that their owners may not know about. Panic buttons are a common security feature on most alarm systems, usually in a fixed location, on the keypad or in a portable transmitter. Another feature common to modern alarm systems enabled with keypads is the **Ambush Code**. This is a special code that is used if the resident is forced by an assailant to enter the home and disengage the alarm. By inputting the ambush code, a silent signal is sent to the alarm company, which immediately dispatches the police to the residence. The monitoring company *will not call* the resident first to determine whether it was a false alarm.

Another important feature is the **Instant Enable**. Most alarms give the user about 30 seconds to a minute to turn off the alarm when entering from the front or garage doors. Instant immediately will trip the alarm if any door is opened – including the front or garage doors, which usually have delayed alarm functions. This feature typically is used when the family or residents are retiring for the evening, and no other family member or resident will be coming in from the outside. Unlike when the Ambush code has been employed, the alarm company will call the home first to determine whether it was a false alarm, or if the police should be dispatched.

With a modern alarm system, a home-based worker can choose to arm only the home office's particular zone, especially if it has a dedicated entrance from the outside. This allows the worker or family to enter the home freely from other entrances while keeping the home office secure. This is an attractive feature if the home officer is working in the evening and wants the office window open – but wants the rest of the home protected.

Test your system monthly to ensure the connection is enabled. The alarm company should respond quickly – usually within two minutes. It's also important to change the batteries in your alarm system as well as any smoke or heat detectors every three years – or more frequently, if needed.

To find an alarm provider in your market, contact the National Burglar and Fire Alarm Association (www.alarm.org).

WHAT IF…?

… you only wanted – or could afford – to protect a single room, like your home office? Mini-alarm systems can be used to protect a single room within a larger home lacking an alarm system. This is ideal for tenants or renters who might not have the money or permission to install a more permanent or high-end alarm. Products such as the Mini Alert or do-it-yourself kits from Radio Shack and other retailers operate with batteries, can be installed quickly, require no new wiring, and easily can be moved to a new location.

WHAT IF…?

… you had a state-of-the-art alarm system, but your home became flooded with carbon monoxide or radon gas? How would you know? Both are colorless, odorless and deadly gases. Radon is a naturally occurring gas that can accumulate in homes. Carbon monoxide (CO) most often comes from a malfunctioning gas oven, space heater, fireplace or chimney when fumes couldn't be properly vented to the outside. CO kills nearly 1,500 Americans each year. If your home has any of these appliances or features, or if you are in a region that has radon, place one alarm on every floor and near sleeping areas (the cost: $50 to $100 each). As with all alarm systems, test the radon and CO monitors and sensors frequently. While you're at it, test the home for lead and asbestos.

NOTES:

NOTES:

CHAPTER III
SECURING THE HOME OFFICE INSIDE

Chapter Overview: Securing the home office inside is as important as protecting the exterior and property. This chapter will discuss how to prevent theft by burglars, or tampering, snooping or inadvertent damage by the family, boarders or guests.

Imagine if someone were to get into your home and home office. Are your documents – and your client's important or even confidential files – safe from harm? Protecting your personal and business property and files is an important element of home office security. It *must* be considered as part of the home office's Emergency Action Plan, and it *must* be continually addressed to ensure content protection is updated. Often we back up documents or hard drives every few months, or neglect to log the serial numbers of expensive hardware, expecting that we'll get to it *eventually*. Break-ins, thefts, fires and other emergencies happen regardless of our preparedness. Therefore, being prepared requires constant attention.

Once the outside and perimeter are secure, then move indoors to protect valuables and confidential documents and information. In fact, protecting the home and home office should be a simultaneous effort.

> ## WHAT IF...?
>
> ... you see broken glass, an open door or damaged doorframe at your home? Never enter the home or peer in the windows or doorway. Use your mobile phone or a neighbor's phone to call the police – and stay out of harm's way until the police arrive.

INVENTORY YOUR POSSESSIONS

If a burglar hit your home and had the time to clean you out, do you know how much you would lose? Whether you're protecting your space from theft or preparing to increase your business insurance coverage, you should have a complete inventory of your belongings. Your inventory should include still and video images, as well as a complete written log of your possessions, encompassing both business equipment, as well as personal property.

Start by walking through your home and making a list of all your valuable possessions and property. The written inventory should include receipts for any purchases, including computers and other technology, software, office furniture, and anything that an insurance company might be required to reimburse you for in case of a loss. Serial numbers should be logged whereever possible. Your name or other identifying marks should be written on in permanent marker or engraved on all valuable possessions as well. Do *not* include your social security number; that number should be closely guarded and protected. Instead, use your driver license number, including the two-letter state designation to help trace the origin of any property. If you do not have a driver license, apply for a state identification card, which will have its own distinctive number.

Property that cannot be engraved or marked – like antiques, china, certain jewelry or other products – should be cataloged in

SECURING THE HOME OFFICE INSIDE

detail in your list of possessions, and photographed closely, making sure to include any special identifying features.

A possible list of business and personal possessions would include:

- Computer hardware and peripherals (including printers, scanners, battery backups, monitors, and multimedia accessories).
- Fax machine, business telephone system (including desktop and portable units).
- Cameras, lenses and other photography equipment.
  Office furniture (desk, chair, file cabinets, guest seating, etc.)
- Valuable items such as jewelry, art, antiques, collectibles, televisions, VCRs, stereos, small appliances, bicycles.
- Financial documents, including bonds and stocks certificates.
- Automobiles, motorcycles, boats or other motorized vehicles on the premises.

WHAT IF...?

... the videotape of your "valuables" didn't include your files, photographs and other items with little or no quantifiable valuation – but nonetheless still are important? Your video record also should include a walk-through of your office and workspace, making sure to record essential elements of your filing system.

Using the video camera, walk through the home and home office. Remember to talk while taping; include mention of the date. Creating a narrative of what you're videotaping will provide backup to your written list of belongings. Using the list you've written up and a still-image camera, photograph all of those same possessions. If your camera has the feature, insert the date stamp onto the images. This makes submission of claims for individual items easier than if you had only the entire videotape.

Make two copies of the tape and the photographs, and print a copy of the complete inventory. One batch should be stored onsite in the family or business safe. The other should be stored off site at a friend or family member's home, a friend's business location or in a safe-deposit box at your bank. Remember to update the inventory, and refile the document and supporting receipts whenever any new items are purchased.

SAFES & OTHER LOCKING STORAGE DEVICES

A safe is a valuable protective measure to have around the home and home office. It can protect everything from jewelry to important personal papers to client files and electronic media.

When considering which safe to buy, first know your needs. Some safes are designed for paperwork but cannot withstand the high temperatures to safely protect digital media like diskettes or videotapes. In a fire, any of these products stored in such a safe could be destroyed (this possibility also is a good reason to store duplicates of sensitive or important files off site). fireproof media safes, or "composite" safes, are designed to store these belongings safely, providing protection against high temperatures for a longer duration than non-fireproof media safes.

Before making your purchase, you'll need to know how much you likely will be storing in the safe. Make a list of the type and amount of contents you intend to place in your safe. Beyond business files and media, such a list could include jewelry, stocks and

SECURING THE HOME OFFICE INSIDE

bonds and other essential documents, cash and firearms. Knowing how much you'll need to store will aid in your selection.

A variety of safes is available, and these range in size and shape. Protection ranges from fire to the sophisticated tools of the experienced burglar. Floor or wall safes or a vault can be hidden from view. Large, stand-alone safes are more obvious and in plain view – but also can be daunting in their size and appearance. Stand-alone safes often have holes or marks in the bottom for drilling and bolting to the floor or other heavy or awkward objects. Some burglars will labor to walk away with a 100-pound safe – just to take the chance that something valuable is inside. Implementing this precaution can provide more deterrence to the burglar.

Here's a listing of the most common varieties of safes, and their typical uses. Their applications and prices vary by need – generally anti-theft or fire protection. Generally, safes can be purchased from $100 up to several thousand dollars, depending on the need, size and protective ability.

- Anti-burglar safes: These don't provide as much fire or heat protection, instead emphasizing on theft prevention. Most safe manufacturers subscribe to a rating system, and most safes are rated according to their resistance to burglar's tools, including torches, saws, chisels and the like. TL ratings refer to burglar "tools"; TR ratings refer to burglar torches. TRTL ratings address use of both. Any rating accompanied by an X6 means the safe meets that rating for all six sides. A TL15-rated safe is designed to thwart the average burglar using average tools for up to 15 minutes; a TL30 is designed to resist entry for around 30 minutes.
- Fire safes: From the small locking box to a larger model, these are designed to protect paperwork and digital or electronic media up to 1,700 degrees. Theft protection is not their primary goal; if you need both, consider a more expensive unit that combines theft and fire protection.

- Composite safes: These are designed to protect contents both from burglar tools and fire damage. With protected hinges and flame-resistant mechanisms, they can temporarily thwart a burglar's attempts to crack the safe, and protect valuable media from high temperatures.
- Media or "data" safes: These are created for offices or home offices that need protection for floppy disks, backup tapes, CD-ROMs, computer diskettes and other electronic media storage products. They are designed to maintain internal temperature below approximately 125 degrees and internal humidity below 80 percent. This helps protect against destruction or corruption of the data stored on the media. The longer the exposure to extreme temperature, the higher the likelihood of damage of the media. These should not be considered a single resource for media storage. Remove a separate back-up copy of sensitive data to another safe location, like a neighbor or friend's home, or a bank safe deposit box.

Locking and Fireproof File Cabinets

A wise safety regimen calls for protecting valuable contents, sensitive media and critical data and files of all kinds. Use of a locking and/or fireproof file cabinet can help protect files and other contents too large for the average in-home safe.

UL-rated insulated file cabinets are rated for both fire and impact protection. Depending on the model, some units can protect files against direct fire damage for up to several hours, as well as limit compromise from direct impact from falling debris or a fall caused by collapse of the floor the unit is housed on. As with traditional file cabinets, fireproof models vary by size and capacity. Although you may currently use a four-drawer file cabinet for all your filing needs, protecting all that content from a fire may not be necessary. As with other protective measures, survey your inventory of sensitive files and buy the unit that can serve the capacity you require.

SECURING THE HOME OFFICE INSIDE

Locking Desk Drawers

Couple the use of a safe and locking file cabinet with a locking desk drawer. It isn't always necessary to lock everyday items – such as the company or personal checkbook, deposits, cash, bills, receipts and check stubs – in the home office safe or locking file cabinet, especially if you use these items often. A locking desk drawer can be used to store these items close at hand, but provide the security and peace of mind from knowing they're easily locked away when you're not around. A key lock can be installed permanently into the desk drawer by a professional, or you can install a latch and use a padlock to secure the drawer.

PROTECTION FROM THE LITTLEST INTRUDERS

If children live in your home, then your office should be child-proofed. Without intending to, children can cause much havoc by pulling plugs and wires, ferreting through files, playing with the computer keyboard or CPU, and even eating or drinking in the home office when the home officer is not around.

Such innocent events can lead to severe risk to the business, its data and company operations. Simple childproofing measures can help ensure your home office is protected from the little ones.

Consider these effective tools and practices to keep kids out of your expensive or sensitive areas – and in turn keep the youngsters themselves protected:

- Tower enclosure and wire chases: A computer tower enclosure should include a door that can help keep little fingers from exploring the CPU, its colorful buttons and the nest of wires in the back. A lock may not be required; with the door closed, some children will look no farther. If a simple lock is needed, a strap of Velcro ® could suffice. If more is needed, visit a hardware store for a simple latch and lock. Wire chases similarly can hide otherwise alluring wires.

This can help keep children from pulling on wires, and prevent pets and children from becoming entangled in them.
- Locking desk drawers: A single locking drawer can be used to store important contents, such as the company checkbook, backed-up data, even the wallet or cash that otherwise would be lying around on the desktop.
- Locking file cabinet: Some locking file cabinets secure only one drawer; some secure them all. Decide how many files you need protected (the more drawers that lock generally the more expensive the unit will be). You may need only one drawer's worth of files protected.
- Closet door locks: Many home office closets are among the most important spaces in the enterprise – and the most alluring for a young explorer. Whether the doors are accordion doors that fold open, or bypass doors on tracks, a simple latch affixed high on the door can help keep young children away. For added protection, a hasp with a key or combination lock can further secure the closet.
- Store-bought plastic children's locks. Cabinet, closet and drawer locks designed by such companies as Safety 1st and others are available at children is and toy stores and are effective in childproofing and keeping toddlers out of a variety of cabinetry. Also consider electrical outlet covers.

  Locking the office door: Whether you have a deadbolt or use the handle knob lock, preventing access is one way to prevent disaster. This may seem extreme. To parents of active children, a locked office door would help avoid snooping, rummaging through files, or even accidental damage to computers ("What's the green button on daddy's computer do?"). Parents can leave the home office with peace of mind knowing they won't return to chaos perpetrated by their kids – or their kids' visiting friends.
- No surfing zone. If the computer is for business, decide whether older children should be allowed to surf the Internet, receive email or download files to the system. Not

only will they become accustomed to surfing on the computer – even when the parent would like to be working, and thereby creating potential conflicts – the possibility of downloading a virus is increased.
- Review the rules: Depending on the child, even young kids can be told what's on and off limits. Starting sometime when they are between two and three years of age, sit down and discuss what mommy or daddy do from this room called the home office. Tell the children why they must listen to and follow the rules. Sometimes telling children that what parents do from the home office helps buy toys, videos, snacks or clothes helps them comprehend the importance of listening to these rules.

PERSONAL AND DESKSIDE SAFETY SUPPLIES

If you commonly work at home without family around, your safety could be heightened by keeping a clutch of security items on hand. Although you'd generally be advised to meet first-time or even repeat clients off site (see Chapter IV about alternative meeting locations), when meeting clients at home, personal protection should always be paramount. Depending on the local ordinances or laws, keeping the portable phone, a can of personal defense spray, a handheld alarm panic button, or a personal audible alarm (which emits a loud sound when pressed) close by can bolster your sense of security.

Whether it's a power black-out at night, or something stirring in your house at any hour, your safety and security could be aided by having a few simple tools on hand. These items can be kept at your workstation, on a shelf or in a desk drawer – without taking up much room. But they'll provide peace of mind while you work alone.

- Flashlight: Select a small but powerful penlight for easy storage, or a larger model that will project a bright and wide beam to illuminate a large area. Halogen flashlights provide a brighter light than most incandescent flashlight bulbs. Make sure the batteries are fresh to ensure it's ready when you need it. Place several flashlights throughout the home, including the office, the bedside table and the kitchen.

- Portable phone: A cordless phone will provide mobility in case you need to leave your home office to investigate a noise, or if you feel threatened. The desktop phone should have programmed into speed dial the phone numbers of several neighbors or friends you would call in case of an emergency.

- Cellular phone: If someone were attempting to break into your home, he could cut your phone lines to keep you or your alarm system from calling out for help. Having your cellular phone charged and on hand provides a reliable lifeline to the world outside. (Helpful hint: Even if your cellular phone is kept in the car or shared by someone else in your home, if you have older model cell phones lying around, that could help create a safety net. Many phones, when charged, are designed to allow a caller to dial 911 – even if they don't have service on the unit.)

- Personal audible alarm: These devices gained favor in the mid-1990s. Although they're not so common now as then, they still can provide added security. When activated, these handheld alarms emit a loud siren-type alarm; some have a lighting mechanism that flashes brightly in case the user is outdoors.

- Stun gun: Used correctly and only in the event of eminent physical threat to the owner, these handheld personal security devices can temporarily stun or immobilize an assailant. Battery-powered, they require the user to make physical contact with the intended target. These are unlawful in some municipalities; check with your city or county police department or clerk's office to determine whether they're legal in your area. As with any defense tool, these are

SECURING THE HOME OFFICE INSIDE

powerful weapons. Learn to use it properly, and be certain that if you brandish it that it won't be taken from – and used against – you. Store safely and keep away from children.

- Mace: Whether you get the Mace® brand self-defense spray, or a mustard, pepper or other handheld defense spray, keeping a bottle near your workstation can provide quick defense against an intruder, or an attacking dog if you're outside. Beware of keeping these and any defense products where children can reach and activate them.

- A fire escape or rope ladder for offices or rooms on floors above ground level: Home offices on a second or higher floor might have their access blocked in a fire. The height could cause injury of the worker or resident who had to jump to safety. A simple rope ladder stored in the office or outside the window can facilitate a quick exit in case of an emergency.

- Fire extinguisher. These are important for any home – and home office. Even if one or several are stored elsewhere in the home, one in the home office can be used to quickly extinguish any electrical or other fires that may break out in or around the workspace. Select an ABC-style model designed to extinguish electrical, flammable liquid, or wood, paper or cloth fires. Make certain to purchase a model designed for general use, as well as on computers and other office equipment. Some chemical elements used in fire extinguishers can permanently damage computer components – even if the fire doesn't.

- First aid kit. A must for any home, it's often overlooked in the home office – especially the home office without children. This should include adhesive bandages, alcohol swabs/antiseptic wipes, Neosporin ointment, surgical dressings, gauze rolls, elastic bandages, surgical gloves, and a bottle of syrup of Ipecac to induce vomiting. Because this kit likely will be used by other household members, inspect it frequently to ensure it remains well-stocked.

NATURAL DISASTER PREPARATION

Each year, from June through November, many American homeowners in Atlantic and Gulf Coast states share one common emotion: angst. Ditto for folks living in Tornado Alley in early spring, Northeasterners in the dead of winter, and probably anyone along an earthquake fault line any time of year.

Hurricanes, tornadoes, nor'easters, blizzards, earthquakes, wildfires and other natural disasters can be hazardous to life and property. But when you run a writing business from home, they're bad for business, too. Although you cannot prevent such calamities, you can mitigate their impact on your home and home office. Realizing that this vulnerability exists – and planning for contingencies and recovery in advance – can help any business limit downtime in the event of a catastrophic event.

These episodes also highlight just how alone people who work from home can be. When a storm or other natural disaster threatens the traditional corporate office, people band together to prepare. Vendors are hired to put up shutters, and the workers inside help one another prepare. After the disaster, people in corporate settings work together to recover. Home officers are on their own – left to do the double-duty of battening down the home and office. What's worse: home workers have to set it all back up again when the threat subsides, hopefully without suffering too much downtime.

Preparation is essential to keeping the business operational, and to ensure clients don't begin to worry either about you – or the status of their projects.

As a storm is approaching is no time to prepare for a hasty exit. Parents might recall the advice given to them before the birth of their first child: Prepare your personal belongings *before* the mother goes into labor. Once labor begins, the mad dash to head for the hospital is no time to fetch and pack the camera, toiletries, clothes

SECURING THE HOME OFFICE INSIDE

and anything else desired for the hospital stay. Similarly, a partially prepared "Evac-Bag" should be on hand in the home office in case a natural disaster strikes. It should include a variety of essential items, including: important, current or archived documents or records; personal and business information, such as client contact data, credit card records and insurance contacts; the cellular phone and charger; personal digital assistant and laptop computer and charger; toiletries; and a change of clothes.

As a matter of course, the home officer should take the following steps when appropriate to ensure the office is prepared in advance of a storm or other disaster (also see the *Home Office Natural Disaster Action Plan* for additional details).

WHAT IF...?

... a storm or other natural disaster struck your home office? What would help you pull through? A positive mental attitude – or PMA – can determine how well your survive just such an episode. Disasters befall even the best of us, often rendering asunder our best-laid plans. How we persevere and thrive amid chaos and challenges can help define whom we are as professionals - and people. At the very least, a hurricane warning can be a good character builder.

Earthquake Preparedness

How prepared is your home office in the event of an earthquake? It might seem as if you can't do much to prepare. But look around your office at the furnishings, cabinets, file cabinets, bookcases, computer equipment and other nonstructural elements. By anchoring or affixing these to the wall or ground, you can limit some of the damage and disarray that even a minor tremor can cause.

Fastening unsecured furniture or equipment to more secure elements can be accomplished simply and quickly. You'll need:

- A drill with a masonry bit for concrete walls, or standard bit for drywall, studs or wood.
- A screwdriver and/or screwdriver bit for the drill.
- Masonry screws to affix the bracket to walls.
- Mollies or anchors to affix brackets to drywall.
- Metal L or Z brackets to brace furniture to other fixed objects.
- Velcro®, two-sided tape and/or museum glue.

The L brackets should be positioned around the perimeter of the cabinet or bookcase. Depending on the style of cabinet or bookcase, drill through the unit and affix it directly to the wall behind it. Use screws that are long enough to anchor securely into the unit, but not too long as to punch through the back of the unit. Two or more large file cabinets can be secured together to provide additional stability.

For cabinets with doors, install door latches, self-locking mechanisms, or simple childproof locks to keep doors from opening during a tremor. For cabinets with no doors, keep items from falling out of or off shelves by installing a plastic, wood or metal lip or barrier across the front of each shelf. To provide more stability and a lower center of gravity, place heavier items on lower shelves. Use hot glue, museum gel or Velcro® to affix loose decorative items, such as planters, fishbowls, or knick-knacks to shelves. In addition to picture hooks, use two-sided or double-stick tape to secure pictures or plaques to walls. For heavier items, install screw eyes into the wall, and thread the frame's picture wire through the eye.

Securing the computer, peripherals and other home office electronics requires several approaches. Use L brackets with adhesive, Velcro® or two-sided tape to anchor the computer CPU to the

SECURING THE HOME OFFICE INSIDE

desk. Use Velcro® to secure the monitor, fax machine, printer, battery backup, phone and other peripherals or accessories to the desktop. Stereos and televisions also should be secured.

Home Office Natural Disaster Action Plan

This document has been prepared to outline the steps to be taken to prevent or minimize damage to the home office, its contents or the ability to perform or conduct business in the event of a natural disaster or act of God. Those are identified as hurricanes, tornadoes, earthquakes, winter storms and wildfires. (See Chapter II for more detail).

1. ___ The home office itself has been secured as well as possible against structural, water, wind or other damage. Windows have storm shutters or plywood to be installed before a windstorm. Locking desk drawers, file cabinets and closet locks protect nonessential items. Computers and other valuable technology also are addressed (as noted below).

2. ___ The Evac-Bag has been prepared, including essential documents and supplies: important business files; active files backed up to diskette from the computer; the laptop computer (and charger); cellular phone (and charger); the personal digital assistant; personal and business information, such as client contact data, credit card records and insurance contacts; a flashlight; toiletries; and a change of clothes (if necessary).

3. ___ The 72-hour kit also is ready. This extension of the Evac-Bag includes food, water, medicines, warm clothes, blankets and other supplies. The car should be filled with fuel, and the family or person ready to evacuate if necessary.

4. ___ Important documents and computer files have been backed up, wrapped in plastic and placed in a locking drawer, file cabinet or fireproof safe.

5. ___ The video or photographic inventory and accompanying list of serial numbers for all electronic equipment (computer, laptop computer, printer, fax machine, scan-

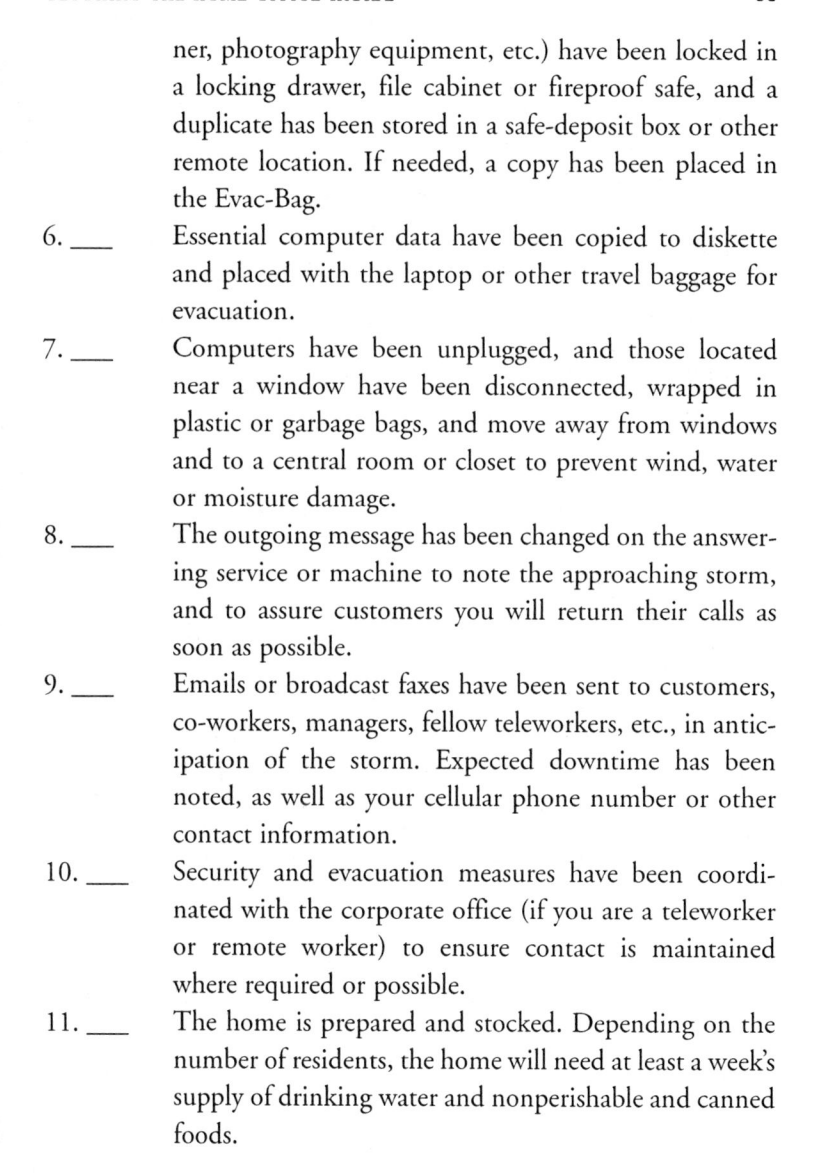

SECURING THE HOME OFFICE INSIDE

ner, photography equipment, etc.) have been locked in a locking drawer, file cabinet or fireproof safe, and a duplicate has been stored in a safe-deposit box or other remote location. If needed, a copy has been placed in the Evac-Bag.

6. ___ Essential computer data have been copied to diskette and placed with the laptop or other travel baggage for evacuation.

7. ___ Computers have been unplugged, and those located near a window have been disconnected, wrapped in plastic or garbage bags, and move away from windows and to a central room or closet to prevent wind, water or moisture damage.

8. ___ The outgoing message has been changed on the answering service or machine to note the approaching storm, and to assure customers you will return their calls as soon as possible.

9. ___ Emails or broadcast faxes have been sent to customers, co-workers, managers, fellow teleworkers, etc., in anticipation of the storm. Expected downtime has been noted, as well as your cellular phone number or other contact information.

10. ___ Security and evacuation measures have been coordinated with the corporate office (if you are a teleworker or remote worker) to ensure contact is maintained where required or possible.

11. ___ The home is prepared and stocked. Depending on the number of residents, the home will need at least a week's supply of drinking water and nonperishable and canned foods.

HOME OFFICE NATURAL DISASTER CONTACT LIST

These individuals *must be* contacted before and after the home office enters *Natural Disaster Preparation Mode.* They include clients and customers; essential vendors; fellow teleworkers, managers, direct reports and corporate clients; business partners and strategic allies; and others who must know the home officer's whereabouts. This contact list also can be used to notify these individuals of any plans for extended travel. Once the storm passes or the threat subsides, these individuals must be called again to alert them to the business's operational state and the status of any scheduled projects.

Contact Name _____
Phone Number(s) _____
Email _____ *Contact made?* Y   N

Contact Name _____
Phone Number(s) _____
Email _____ *Contact made?* Y   N

Contact Name _____
Phone Number(s) _____
Email _____ *Contact made?* Y   N

Contact Name _____
Phone Number(s) _____
Email _____ *Contact made?* Y   N

Contact Name _____
Phone Number(s) _____
Email _____ *Contact made?* Y   N

Contact Name _____
Phone Number(s) _____
Email _____ *Contact made?* Y   N

SECURING THE HOME OFFICE INSIDE

Contact Name _____
Phone Number(s) _____
Email _____ *Contact made?* Y   N

Contact Name _____
Phone Number(s) _____
Email _____ *Contact made?* Y   N

Contact Name _____
Phone Number(s) _____
Email _____ *Contact made?* Y   N

Contact Name _____
Phone Number(s) _____
Email _____ *Contact made?* Y   N

Contact Name _____
Phone Number(s) _____
Email _____ *Contact made?* Y   N

Contact Name _____
Phone Number(s) _____
Email _____ *Contact made?* Y   N

Contact Name _____
Phone Number(s) _____
Email _____ *Contact made?* Y   N

Contact Name _____
Phone Number(s) _____
Email _____ *Contact made?* Y   N

Contact Name _____
Phone Number(s) _____
Email _____ *Contact made?* Y   N

Contingency plans also should include a list of peers, friends or associates whom you can call on in case your office is hit by a storm or disaster. For example, when Hurricane Andrew struck Miami in 1992, areas just 30 miles to the north were only slightly damaged. Many companies and independent workers temporarily moved and resumed their operations in an unaffected area.

Each year, call your insurance agent to review your homeowner's policy, content limits and business coverage. Inquire about increasing coverage on business equipment. The typical homeowners policy covers dwelling contents as a percentage of the appraised value of the home. Often, this excludes or caps business computers or electronic equipment. An inexpensive business insurance rider may increase equipment coverage – and add to peace of mind. Also, consider purchasing business interruption insurance. This covers downtime if the business is disabled by a storm, fire or other disaster.

Insurance issues to consider include:

- Raising content limits: Typical insurance covers dwelling contents as a percentage of the appraised value of the home. Often, this excludes or caps jewelry, electronics or computers. An inexpensive insurance rider may increase equipment coverage.
- Buying business-interruption insurance: This covers downtime if the business is closed by a storm or fire. Beware: Some insurers don't provide this coverage for the home office.
- Buying business owners coverage: This policy allows business owners to insure to value, increasing coverage as potential losses increase. The policy often requires a business to insure 80 percent of what the company is worth. Penalties often exist, if the owner doesn't meet that requirement.

NOTES:

NOTES:

CHAPTER IV
HABITS TO IMPROVE SAFETY & SECURITY

Chapter Overview: Often, hiding your home-based workstyle can help avoid any chance or criminal intrusion or other threat. This chapter will delve into ways to ensure your work habits don't become a spectacle – or at least something outsiders can come to count on if they're looking for a person or residence to victimize.

Humans are creatures of habit. Our lives become patterns of daily activities that we repeat with such regularity and predictability that an observer often could set a watch by our timeliness and habitual behavior. For the at-home worker, it's no different. We often awaken around the same time, power up the computer, head out for the newspaper or mail, take our morning or afternoon walk or bike ride and power down the computer or monitor at night. Our kids get home at a certain hour. Our spouse arrives home from work after the daily commute. If we telework, our days away often are set as if in stone from week to week.

Now, imagine you're a burglar watching all this predictable behavior. This kind of patterning would be blissful – a beautiful mix of timing and expected events that would make a break-in simple to pull off.

For that reason, it's important for at-home workers to alter the predictable patterns of their lives, mask the fact that they work from home, and take every opportunity to shield the person and enterprise from attack. Besides, being unpredictable can be fun and invigorating.

NEVER LET 'EM SEE YOU WORKING

Who knows you work from home? Whom do you want to know?

Some at-home workers are open about their chosen workplace. Others are quiet about it. Whether it's fear of violating a municipal ordinance forbidding home-based work, or concern about neighbors and others knowing they're home during the day, some workers feel that the fewer people who know about their chosen workplace, the better. Even if you tell all your clients, colleagues, friends and others that you work from home, that doesn't mean you want strangers to know. The way you treat your business appearance can determine who – if anyone – knows where you work.

Again, wearing the hat of the Chief Security Officer, treat your home office more like your home than an office. If your home is your castle, protect it, yourself and your privacy by employing tactics designed to conceal your work-at-home reality.

Are you a creature of habit? Suburban neighborhoods already are the prime hunting grounds of thieves and burglars who know that the community homes and streets are quiet and empty once the commuting masses have headed to work each morning. Those same criminals often stake out neighborhoods to detect people's routines. If they catch you in some predictable routine – like your morning walk or even just fetching the paper at a set time – that could make you a prospect ripe for attacking. Limit the signs that you work from home:

- Don't let multiple newspapers, flyers, business correspondence or overnight parcels accumulate near the front door or in the yard. Fetch them as soon as you see them arrive. Parcels by the front door are a telltale sign that a business is being run from the residence.

HABITS TO IMPROVE SAFETY & SECURITY

- Retrieve your mail soon after it's delivered, or install a mail slot in your front door. As with most businesses, home-based companies or teleworkers' home offices often get more mail than a traditional residence. Mailboxes stuffed with mail – where the mailbox doors are bulging out or left plainly open – are a sign that no one may be around.
- Be unpredictable. Do you get your newspaper at 8:45 each morning, take your morning stroll at 10:30, head for the mailbox at 2 in the afternoon? The more irregular your schedule is, the less likely anyone will know to target you. Lock the door each time you re-enter the home, especially if your home office doesn't have a view of the front yard or the approach to your front door.

Protecting or disguising your space is another trick to ensure your home office is hidden from view, both literally and metaphorically. One emerging trend for the home officer and small business owner – and even a teleworker – is to rent space in a local executive suite or executive business center. These facilities are an increasingly common alternative to the home office address. Users rent an actual space to work from, or sign up for a "Business Identity Program," which provides the user with a street and suite address that then become the user's primary business mailing address. A receptionist can answer calls in the company name, and sign for packages. To any outsider, the address and telephone answering appear as if it's the company's main facility.

Teleworkers use "Telework Centers" as an alternative to the busy – or even secluded – home office. These facilities have all the trappings of the corporate office – the private phone number, the high-speed Internet connection, the mail service and private workspace. They provide a safe and secure workspace buzzing with remote employees and teleworkers from other companies.

Here are several more tricks to masking the home office within:

- Rent a post office box. When you work from home, your business card is no place for your home address. Costing about $25 every six months, a post office box provides an acceptable business address to put on stationery. Because many shipping services won't deliver to post office boxes, consider using the address of a local pack-and-ship storefront, such as MailBoxes Etc. or U.S. Pak & Ship, or an executive suite or business center (as mentioned above) for your stationery. Just remember that Postal Service regulations require the PMB (private mail box) or "#" be used on all your stationery and arriving correspondence to denote such services. This can hinder your professional appearance.
- Make your space appear corporate. When writing your address or ordering stationery, call Apt. B-101, for example, "Suite" or "No." B-101. Or add "Suite 100" to your street address if you live in a single-family home. It appears more like a business than a residential address, and can throw off someone looking for a residence to target for burglary.
- Use your surname and first initial in the telephone directory and on the nameplate for your condo or apartment building. This will help conceal your gender.
- Don't include your address in your telephone listing. It's important for a business to have its phone number listed. Your address need not be included. If a client or vendor needs your address, they'll call. Then you can screen the caller before providing the information. If you have any concerns, provide your post office box or arrange with a friend in a traditional corporate office to receive your overnight or courier packages.
- Use caller ID to screen incoming calls. If you don't recognize or if they seem suspicious, let the answering machine or voicemail answer the call. Then screen the call or listen to the message.

HABITS TO IMPROVE SAFETY & SECURITY

- Participate in neighborhood crime watches, or at least get to know your neighbors. This raises your prominence in the community and increases the likelihood they will keep an eye out for you.

PROTECTION FROM HOME INVASION

You know your usual delivery people. They arrive in marked vehicles, wear company uniforms, and if you've been working from home for any length of time, you're probably on a first-name basis.

But what if a new driver shows up one day – out of uniform and in street clothes – and requests a signature on a parcel? Even if you have standing instructions with the company authorizing parcels to be left without a signature, what if he insists? What's worse, some delivery companies – and especially couriers – drive unmarked cars or vans. Should you open the door?

Common sense and safety protocols would suggest not to. The same is true for utility, telephone or city maintenance personnel asking that you open the door, or even sales people or solicitors looking to make their pitches. Although their intentions most often are benign, we are left wondering about when to open our doors – and when to play it safe – because of the pervasive criminal element.

Home invasion is on the rise. Would-be criminals masquerading as repairmen, delivery drivers or other everyday service personnel beg our attention to a pressing matter – hoping we'll let our guard down for just a moment so they can gain entry into our homes or home offices.

What are the most common tricks?

- Gas leak. "There's a gas leak in the area, and we need to check your residence."
- Phone or electrical service. "We've had a report of outages or service breaks in the area. We need to check your line or service."

- Flower or gift delivery. "Special delivery for the resident. Can you please sign?"
- Sales solicitation. "We have a special office we'd like to discuss with you."

Although knowing when someone at your door is legitimate often is impossible, you can protect yourself with a few simple measures:

- Keep your front door locked.
- Use your peephole or video surveillance camera to see who is at the door; also look for people who might be hiding off to the side or just beyond view. Ask for identification to be held up to the peephole or camera.
- Ask whom they are and why they're there. If their intentions are unclear, or if they stumble through their story, don't open the door.
- If it's a delivery person for a company with whom you have registered standing instructions authorizing the unsigned drop of parcels, tell him to leave the parcel. If he refuses, tell him to call the office to verify instructions are on file.
  If it's a courier or company you don't recognize or don't have such instructions for, ask for the corporate phone number, and call to ensure a parcel is scheduled for delivery.
- Ask him his name, service/employee number and supervisor's name, and tell him you will call their employer to inquire whether a service technician has been dispatched.
- Look up the number yourself; do not use any number he provides.
- If it's a gift or flower delivery, ask that it be dropped at the door. If he insists on a signature and you feel uncomfortable opening the door, get the name of the company, look the number up yourself, and tell the company you authorize the delivery person to leave the item at your doorstep.

HABITS TO IMPROVE SAFETY & SECURITY

- Don't answer the door. If you were working in the corporate office environment, you wouldn't be at home to answer the door anyway.

In all instances, keep your door locked. If a delivery person leaves before you can verify his credentials, call the police and report the incident. If the person is there to service the home, and the story checks out with the employer, if you still feel uncomfortable, call a friend to come by and stay around while the technician is in your home. Or send the worker away and have them return when someone will be home with you.

Sometimes, home-invasion robbers will hide in wait for a homeowner to return to the residence. They strike once the homeowner gets to the door. If you have an alarm system, know how to use your assault or ambush feature. By using this code, the homeowner will appear to be disengaging the alarm, when in reality you are transmitting a silent panic alarm to the central station. The alarm company does not call the homeowner to verify the alarm has been set off. Instead, the dispatcher immediately calls the police. Responding police units approach without using their lights or sirens, so any assailant is unaware of their presence.

WORKING WITH STRANGERS

Sometimes, working from home requires a client meeting. But is the home office the best place to stage such a meeting? Although it might be a comfortable place to live and work alone, the home often isn't conducive to holding a corporate meeting. Aside from not having a large enough meeting space, and possibly being barraged by interruptions by kids, dogs, family members, phone calls and the like, do you really want your home office to be scanned or cased by any client who comes through your door?

Liability also is an issue. Homes have their own intrinsic elements that could pose hazards to visitors. Dogs or animals could nip or bite the guest, and a toy, skateboard or other misplaced item could cause a guest to trip and fall. Any resulting injury could lead to ill will, a lawsuit or damages claimed by the client or visitor against you and/or your business. So, if clients are to come over, try to keep them from the family's living areas, or make sure the home has been sufficiently tidied up before their arrival. This also will make a better impression on the client.

> **WHAT IF...?**
>
> ... a first-time guest, customer, client or even prospective employee wants to meet at your home office? Decline. Meet in a local hotel lobby or restaurant, copy center, Kinko's, public library, executive suite or business center, or other public place. It's safer – for both of you. Befriend the property managers and let them know whether this could be a regular event. They might provide perks, better facilities or more attentive service.

When dealing with newcomers, employ some tactics that will eliminate the need to meet people at your residence. If they scoff, tell them corporate policies must be adhered to. If you must meet newcomers at your home-based workspace, create as much separation between home and office as possible to ensure they don't get too great a glimpse into your personal space. This can help establish a stronger, more professional working relationship, and ensure greater safety and security for you. Here are some power tips to meeting first-time guests at your home office:

- Schedule first-time – and possibly follow-up – meeting off site at a neutral location, such as a restaurant, coffeeshop, executive suite or local library. That gives you time to get a feel for clients' and vendors' character. If you never quite get the right vibe, but don't necessarily feel threatened, just

HABITS TO IMPROVE SAFETY & SECURITY

say your office is not set up to handle meetings. If you must meet on site with clients, walk them directly to the office and try to limit access to your home's living areas.

- Ask a neighbor or other at-home worker to drop in during a client visit, if you feel unsure about the client, to "deliver a proposal you've been working on." Or schedule visits when a teenage or adult family member, an employee or intern is in the home. You also can tell the client someone will be stopping by – even if no one really is.
- Listen to your gut. If someone makes you uneasy after an initial meeting, agree only on subsequent meetings in public areas. Or decline to work with them. Your uneasy feelings could hinder your ability to work professionally – resulting in bad workmanship and decreased productivity.

THWARTING FRAUD, IDENTITY THEFT & CLIENT CONFIDENTIALITY

Because you work from home, you don't have to worry about identify theft or client confidentiality, right?

Wrong.

Couple the Internet Age with the volumes of paper that are generated – often with confidential information attached, such as credit card receipts and bills, bank statements, investment information and tax documents – and an identity thief could ruin your finances by ferreting through your garbage. And if you run a home-based business, you're probably tossing double the amount of information that identity thieves thrive on.

Preventing identity theft is important for everyone. According to the Federal Trade Commission, more than half of the complaints it receives involve credit card fraud – and that a card was opened in the complainant's name. More than a quarter of all complaints involve bank fraud, fraudulent loans and government benefits. Other areas of fraud include unauthorized change of address, fraudulent change or application for a copy of a social security number or card, and application for a new or duplicate passport, driver license or state identification card. Often, much of the information needed to pull off these crimes is available in the average home officer's garbage can. According to the FTC, the most complaints came from Los Angeles, Brooklyn, Chicago, Detroit and Miami.

Here are some ways to prevent identity theft and fraud:

- Treat all client files and corporate documents as if they were your own – and required security. When carrying important documents, never leave your briefcase unattended in the car. Never leave important files open on your desk.
- When corresponding with banks, investment firms and state or federal entities about your personal accounts, keep a record of your conversations. Include the date and time of the call, as well as the name of the person with whom you spoke and his direct telephone number, if appropriate.
- If you are mailing information, returns or payments to state or federal agencies, send such correspondence via certified mail/return receipt requested. Note the date of mailing in your datebook or contact management software, so you can contact the agency if you don't receive the receipt within several weeks. Once it is received, file the returned receipt with a copy of the associated correspondence.
- Shred all discarded files and receipts. Credit card receipts, old bank statements, old printouts of client or internal files or documents, direct mail solicitations for credit cards, and purged content from files. If they're not important to you now – but once were, they could be important to someone else.
- Report fraud to the appropriate government agency: the postal inspector, Social Security Administration, the local police or other law enforcement agency, the county district attorney, and the state attorney general's office. If appropri-

ate in the case of an actual theft of a credit card, get a police report. You may need it for your case with the creditor.

> **WHAT IF...?**
>
> ... you needed to create a password or PIN (personal identification number) for a new account or Web site registration? What's your first choice: your mother's maiden name, or the last four digits of your social security number, the same code that sets your house alarm? Get creative. Sure, it may make keeping track of them harder, but the more passwords or PINs you have, the less likely that a thief discovering *one* number will compromise other valued services. Also, whether for your alarm, network or file access, or other purpose, change your password frequently.

If you discover or suspect any fraud related to your personal or business banking or credit card accounts, contact creditors, including the credit card company, bank card issuer, or other organization, to alert them. Request that the account immediately be closed, a new account opened and new cards issued. Destroy the old cards; the credit card company can issue new cards for next-day delivery, or issue a cash advance from a nearby bank if you are traveling or need money immediately. Remember, in most instances you are not required by law to file a notarized fraud affidavit, although the bank or other creditor may request it. Instead, write, sign and submit a written statement, filed along with any supporting documentation, outlining the issue at hand.

ATM cards are even more susceptible to fraud, which can be more damaging to your personal or business accounts. Because the money is taken directly from your account, if you don't know about the unauthorized withdrawals, you could overdraw the account and have no cash on hand. In such a discovery, immediately contact the bank and have the card cancelled.

Notify your bank of any unauthorized withdrawals, checks written on your business or personal account, or missing checks from the checkbook or binder. Have a stop-payment placed on those specific items. If you believe the account may be compromised, close the account and open a new one.

Credit bureaus are more important than most consumers think – or care to believe. They are vital for individuals and businesses seeking funding, and the lenders who provide the financing. They're also among the first to know whether problems are arising with any previous loans or credit card account. You must notify and clear up any existing discrepancies with the bureaus' fraud prevention departments. Contact the leading bureaus (Equifax, Experian [formerly TRW] and Trans Union), and request that your account carry a fraud alert. Then, request that a free copy of your record to ensure the item or activity has been cleared.

Use the following information to contact the credit bureaus if you suspect fraud or unauthorized activity on your business or personal checking, loan or credit card accounts.

- Equifax, P.O. Box 740241, Atlanta, GA 30374-0241. Report fraud: (800) 525-6285. Order a credit report: (800) 685-1111. Web site: www.equfax.com
- Experian (formerly TRW). P.O. Box 9595, Allen, TX 75013-9595. Report fraud: (800) 301-7195. Order a credit report: (888) 397-3742. Web site: www.experian.com
- Trans Union. Fraud Victim Assistance Division. P.O. Box 6790, Fullerton, CA 92634. Report Fraud: (800) 680-7289. Order Credit Report: (800) 888-4213. Web site: www.tuc.com

To learn more, visit the Federal Trade Commission's Identity Theft Web site at www.consumer.gov/sentinel. Consumers can read the law, file complaints, learn about local law enforcement agencies, and learn how to avoid identity theft and Internet fraud. Or, call the FTC at 877-IDTHEFT (877-438-4338).

> ## WHAT IF...?
>
> ... you had information that you needed protected or copyrighted? Some use the "poor man's copyright" by mailing to themselves the content by certified mail – and *not* opening the parcel once received. Another way is to register it with the U.S. Copyright Office (www.loc.gov/copyright). Online services include ZixMail, a secure document delivery, private email and message-tracking service. For $1 a month, the service encrypts information in email messages and attachments safely (www.zixmail.com).

AVOIDING CORPORATE ESPIONAGE

So, you run a small business or work from home every few days, and you've never considered corporate espionage as a threat? Maybe you should.

As working from home becomes more common, the potential lapses in security and resulting vulnerabilities have grown. That has given rise to the opportunity for corporate espionage – where competitors can sense opportunities to steal secrets, data, files, computers or diskettes and damage your organization by using their contents. Whether you're a teleworker, an entrepreneur or consultant who has access to clients' sensitive files, or even a homeowner with checks, credit card records and other important paperwork, ensuring confidential files don't fall into the wrong hands should be an important element in your home-based security protocol.

Securing your paperwork and data files requires a layered approach, involving protection, backup and storage.

- Duplicates of important files, data and contracts should be made. Where appropriate, essential files should be backed up to protect against theft or loss (see Chapter V for a more thorough discussion of backups). Teleworkers' employers might have automatic backup software that conducts daily backups of all files stored in select locations or directories. Inquire if this software is available for the laptop or home office computer.
- Backup diskettes of your computer files and hard drive copies should be stored offsite at a friend's or family member's home or in your bank safe deposit box.
- When not working in the home office, remove and refile important documents so they are not in plain sight, and store client or personal/work confidential files in a locking file cabinet or desk drawer.
- When possible, avoid downloading documents from the corporate network to the laptop or diskette while still in the corporate office. Instead, log on remotely from the home office and then download the desired documents or files. Once the work is completed, upload the content back to the network server. This helps limit the potential for data loss in the event the laptop or diskette are lost or stolen.
- Empty the Recycle Bin. "Deleted" files removed to the Recycle Bin are still accessible either through right or left mouse click, or access through Windows Manager. Copies of deleted files can be restored or viewed by anyone with access to the computer until the Recycle Bin is emptied. As a precautionary measure, permanently delete confidential or sensitive files. Empty the entire bin by hitting Right Mouse Click and then Empty Recycle Bin. Or you can select and highlight specific files for removal. Files deleted from the Recycle Bin are not easily retrievable. (If you acci-

dentally delete a file, you may still have it stored on backup media).
- Beware errant attachments. Computers are not foolproof. If you are emailing an attached file, understand that the email could go to the wrong recipient, or that the wrong attachment could be selected and sent. Information that is strictly confidential or highly sensitive might be more safely transmitted via fax. Alternatively, the file can be stored to digital media and sent via courier or shipping service.
- Install a mailbox with a lock. This enables the mail carrier to deliver the mail through a small slot, but prevents anyone without a key from opening the box and perusing through or taking the contents.
- Use a cross-cut paper shredder to destroy trash copies of documents, credit card receipts or other sensitive papers. If you don't own a shredder, keep sensitive documents in a box or bag and take them to a friend or ally's business location to use their shredder. An alternative is to take those papers to a document storage, archival and destruction firm, where you can pay to have documents shredded.

Installing a deadbolt on the office door will allow you to lock the office when you're not around. This can keep your office off-limits when you're not there to police the space. Redouble your efforts by installing a window lock on your home office window so the workspace won't be vulnerable to outside entry (see Chapter II to learn more).

To many home-based workers, the portable telephone has become an essential power tool. It untethers workers from their desks or home offices, and allows them to take lunch in the kitchen or dining room, to walk to the mailbox, or shoot hoops with the kids – all without missing a call. But who else might be listening in when you hold a conversation on the portable phone with an important client regarding a sensitive issue?

> ## WHAT IF...?
>
> ... you had to transmit a sensitive document to a client or your company? How do you ensure it won't be intercepted? Data-encryption software can help prevent interception and theft by enabling only the sender and intended recipient from being able to open the attached document with the right digital "key." Visit these services and sites to learn more:
>
> - PCGuardian (www.pcguardian.com).
> - NovaStor (www.data-encryption.com).
> - The WinZap Company (www.winzap.com).

A neighbor with a portable phone operating on a similar frequency, or even a nearby baby room monitor's receiver unit, often can pick up conversations held on portable phones. If it's that simple to inadvertently overhear a phone call, imagine what someone deliberately trying to listen in can hear. The telephone can play an important role in thwarting corporate espionage or information leaks. When making calls to clients in which the information will be sensitive, use a traditional desktop land line or non-portable phone to make the call. If you do use a portable phone, select a digital model in the 900 megahertz or gigahertz bands. Look for models that scan for secure channels. These provide greater frequency security for the calls.

To learn more about privacy, security and how the law can protect you, contact the Privacy Rights Clearinghouse (www.privacyrights.org), your state bar association for an attorney specializing in fraud prevention, the Fair Credit Reporting Act or consumer law.

HABITS TO IMPROVE SAFETY & SECURITY

To find out about The Identity Theft Survival Kit from consultant Mari Frank, visit www.identitytheft.org or call 800-725-0807.

INSURING THE SPACE

According to the Independent Insurance Agents of America, approximately 60 percet of in-home businesses are not properly insured, and the lower the income of an in-home business owner, the less likely he or she is to have business coverage. Even the affluent lack comprehensive insurance, with 59 percent of home-based entrepreneurs making more than $50,000 going without adequate business insurance, according to the association's statistics.

Why don't more home-business owners carry proper coverage? Money is not the issue; few in-home business owners note that money was a significant factor in their decision to forgo business insurance, the group says. The problem is more about knowledge than cost. About 44 percent of those without coverage said they didn't buy business insurance because they thought their homeowner's policy covered their home offices. In many cases, that's a bad assumption.

Depending on the policy and carrier, homeowners' umbrella policies cover certain in-home office equipment. But if the hardware is used for business – as opposed to personal – purposes, it often gets disallowed. You may need a business rider that can be attached to your standard residential policy. This will cover some aspects of the home-based business.

Considerations include:

- Contents coverage: insures losses to inventory or stock and business equipment due to theft, breakage, damage from accidents, fires, floods or other natural disasters.
- Liability: insures yourself or your business in case of someone's injury on or around your property.

- Product liability: insures your products against defect, improper performance or incorrect or misunderstood instructions for usage that could cause injury to others.
- Malpractice: protects you against claims of poor workmanship, improper advice or counsel, or other perceived or real errors related to a professional service.
- Business interruption: provides a revenue stream if your business is shut down or work stops due to illness, accident, catastrophe or other factor.

BUSINESS OWNER'S POLICY

Although your business operates from a home office, your standard residential policy often doesn't provide enough – or even *any*, in some instances – coverage to keep you protected against damage, theft or liability. As a small business operating out of a home or other nontraditional workspace, you could qualify for a business owners policy (BOP). This type of policy covers a variety of elements, often including:

- Professional liability: Akin to malpractice insurance, this policy will insure you against claims by clients or customers who find fault in your services rendered.
- Product liability: This coverage will protect you if a product you create or distribute has a defect that causes damage or harm during its use.
- Bodily injury protection: This coverage protects you in case a visitor has a slip-and-fall accident on your property or in your home, or in case a pet injures a visitor.
- Fire damage.
- Computer hardware and data.
- Property theft protection, both on the premises and off.
- Equipment damage and theft.
- Business income and accounts receivable.
- Outdoor signage.

HABITS TO IMPROVE SAFETY & SECURITY

An Incidental Business Occupancies (IBO) endorsement will provide coverage and pay for additional limits for on- and off-premises business property, money and securities, and additional coverage for personal liability and medical payments.

Prices vary for the coverage, depending on carrier, company category and location, and the amount of the deductible. Not all types of coverage are available in all states. The cost can start at around $250 a year. As with most insurance policies, first request quotes for coverage from the agent handling your current homeowner's policy, the local chamber of commerce, your professional trade association, and the National Federation of Independent Business (www.nfib.org). Be sure to request similar coverage and deductibles, and compare rates. The cost and worth of any business policy depend on how detailed your explanation of your product, service, workplace and client interaction is. Working with a professional agent can ensure you include the appropriate coverage areas, and exclude those that are not necessary.

COVERING THE COMPUTER

What's the power tool in your home office? In most offices, it's the computer. But how protected is your system? Many insurance companies now offers computer hardware, software and data insurance to ensure your system is covered in case of theft, damage, corruption or failure. A few are:

- PromiseMark (www.promisemark.com). This company offers an insurance policy and virus service plan that target home and small businesses. For a flat annual fee, micro businesses receive several months of protection from Symantec's Norton AntiVirus software, emergency virus updates, alerts and warnings, and 24-hour technical support. If a virus damages your system, some repair costs are covered.

> ### WHAT IF...?
>
> ... you telework? Who is responsible for insuring your workspace and equipment? Your corporate laptop might not be covered when used outside the corporate office. Your home office might be off-limits to any visitors for liability reasons. Discuss it with your employer, the human resources department and the executive who oversees company insurance programs.

- Safeware (www.safeware.com). This computer insurance agency claims that 1.2 million computers were stolen, damaged or destroyed in 1999 alone. Safeware offers computer insurance that covers claims for damages related to theft, lightning strikes, power surges and other maladies to hardware, software and peripherals. Premiums start at around $50 a year.
- Your insurance provider. Inquire with your homeowner's or renter's insurance carrier about coverage for your desktop and laptop computers.

NOTES:

NOTES:

NOTES:

CHAPTER V
COMPUTER, LAPTOP & DATA SECURITY & PROTECTION

Chapter Overview: Personal computers are the power tool of the home officer. Lose that tool, and not only is an expensive piece of hardware lost, but so too could be invaluable data and information stored on it. This section will lay out the most important elements of computer system protection.

Personal computers never have been more powerful and essential to the business community – including the at-home worker – than they are today. And home office computers have never been more vulnerable. Between business travel, laptop computer portability and even always-on Internet connections, reports of computer theft, hacking, content corruption and general intrusion from the world and Net outside have become commonplace. And with no corporate IT security department on standby to ensure your computer technology and data are protected, it's up to you – the multitasking home officer – to wear that hat as well.

Home and personal computer protection must encompass a multifaceted approach. Not only are computers susceptible to theft on the road or from within the home office, but Internet connections allow hackers to steal content – without your even knowing about the intrusion.

BATTERY BACKUP & SURGE PROTECTION

People will invest hundreds or even thousand of dollars in scanners, printers, cameras and other expensive peripherals. But what about a battery backup device and simple surge protector? Imagine spending hours writing a document, preparing a proposal or creating a graphic design, and suddenly losing power to your residence. A battery backup or uninterrupted power supply (UPS) could be the answer.

A UPS is designed to supply a constant, even flow of power to your computer in a power outage. This includes a "brown-out," which is a temporary loss of power – which often is just enough to cause a computer to reset and lose any data or content in its RAM (random access memory). UPS systems also include a fuse, which further protects the computer from power surges, spikes and lightning strikes or high-voltage surges from outside sources.

UPS systems come in a variety of styles and prices. Models usually are selected by the amount of time they will provide power to the computer in a power outage. Most will supply a steady stream of power for up to 10 minutes. When the power fails, the UPS emits an audible alarm to alert the computer user that the computer is drawing from battery power. The user then has time to save data, close all open applications, and safely shut down the computer. This style of UPS typically costs less than $100.

UPS systems come with several electrical outlets on the back, into which you can plug your computer terminal and monitor. Most companies do not recommend plugging scanners, printers and other peripherals into the units, as those non-essential devices will drain power from the battery more quickly. Some UPS units also provide phone jacks to protect the computer modem from power surges over the telephone line.

Surge protectors provide a line of defense between your computer and other expensive electronic equipment and power surges and lightning strikes. Surge protectors have a small fuse in line, which is destroyed in the event of a surge of electricity. This prevents the power spike from reaching the computer or other equipment.

> ## WHAT IF...?
>
> ... you suddenly lost power? Would you lose all the data on your computer's active memory? Even if you use a battery backup, make sure your computer performs a backup save every few minutes, and that you frequently perform a hard save to ensure your content is safe. To set your AutoRecovery in Microsoft Word, hit: Alt + Tools, Options, then hit the Save tab. Near the bottom is the option box: Save AutoRecover info every: ___. Your options are from 0 minutes to 120 minutes. Depending on your preference, you can set your AutoRecover to suit your needs, with some users selecting from five to 15 minutes.

Unlike a UPS, surge protectors offer no independent power supply, and cannot be relied upon for power in a black-out or brown-out. They are ideal to protect printers, scanners, fax machines and other expensive electronics, such as telephone systems, televisions, VCRs and stereos.

As with some UPS models, some surge protectors also come equipped with telephone jacks. Users plug the phone wire coming from the wall into the protector, and then a wire coming from the protector plugs into the phone itself. These can help protect expensive telephone equipment from power surges, electrical spikes or lightning strikes carried over the telephone line. Similarly, dedicated surge and lightning strike protectors are available to protect digital, dataline and broadband communications equipment, including modems, routers and hubs. These devices, from companies like American Power Conversion Corp. (www.apcc.com) protect the communications connection, as well as the computer to which the hardware is connected.

VIRUS PROTECTION

It happened to Microsoft. It happened to Yahoo! and eBay. It happens to corporations worldwide. It's the computer virus or the computer hacker. And it can happen to you.

Ramon, Melissa, Little Devina – computer viruses, Trojans and worms are created and intended to cause malice to the unsuspecting user. That's why they're often referred to as malware. Thus, antivirus and hacking protection has emerged as a priority in the digital age. A computer virus is a "bug" designed to "infect" other computers (networks, stand-alone systems and laptops), personal digital assistants, and even cellular or mobile phones. A VBS virus, such as the one in winter 2001 proclaiming "Here you have, ;o)" and promising an image of Anna Kournikova, is a worm that self-propagated by mass mailing itself to everyone in a recipient's Microsoft Outlook address book.

Sometimes a virus just causes systems to lose efficiency and perform sluggishly; sometimes they cause significant damage to the entire computer or even the network the PC is running on. Users then can unwittingly pass along the virus through email or network connections to other computers, thereby passing along the bug. Worms are bits of computer code that snake through the Internet on their own, unbeknownst to computer users. Trojans take their name from the Trojan Horse, a hollow wooden transport used by the Greeks to launch troops inside ancient Troy. In modern terms, this is a destructive application that comes to users posed as a harmless email, correspondence or attachment.

Hacking is the illegal entry by a computer user into another computer or network system. The hacker silently gains entry via the Internet, and then often can access any files on the violated system's hard drive. The hacker can just look around, steal data, or corrupt the entire system. How much damage a hacker or a virus cause is dependent upon two factors: How malicious the hacker or creator of the virus intended the incursion to be, and how you – the target or infected system owner – prepared for the possibility of an attack or reacts to the exposure.

Your exposure to – or protection from – viruses and hacking often is up to you. Free and for-fee tools exist to present an effective defense against most hacking and virus exposure. By installing firewall products and anti-virus software designed to keep hackers and bugs at bay, you often can protect your system and data – and, by extension, the systems and data of those with whom you correspond or to whom you send email or share files.

These are not foolproof, and require frequent updating as new viruses are discovered and new remedies are created. As in protecting your home office, a layering effect tends more effectively to thwart undesired intrusions into your computer. Install and use a firewall product and anti-virus software to protect your system. Then update both constantly – or at least according to the manufacturer's recommendations. Heed the words of warning from computer security expert Bruce Schneier with Counterpane Internet Security (www.schneier.com) and author of *Secrets & Lies: Digital Security in a Networked World*: "Security is a process, not a product."

ANTI-VIRUS PROTECTION

Anti-virus protection can be one of the most important – and one of the simplest to implement – applications for your computer. Viruses can be introduced to a system in many ways, especially Internet downloads, floppy or high-capacity diskettes, CD-ROM, or over a network. The most common method of introduction is via email – if only because it's the most commonly used method of connecting with and receiving information from the networked world outside. Whether purchased from your local software or office supply store or downloaded from the Internet, once installed, anti-virus software should become part of your active toolbar. That way, each application, file or email you download or load on to your computer from a diskette or other media automatically is scanned for viruses. Anti-virus programs should:

- Scan in-bound email or software loaded to the hard drive or RAM memory.
- Alert the user to any viruses or questionable elements found.
- Quarantine the questionable content, or delete the content and cease the application.
- Remain active in the background to be constantly scanning for and protecting the computer or network from potentially harmful content.

Among the most common products on the market are:

- McAfee VirusScan. McAfee's Macro Hunter and ViruLogic technology can safeguard your computer from a variety of viruses, and inform you of newly created viruses and remedies. It scans all potential sources of entry, including email and attachments, Internet downloads, shared files, floppy disks, online services, network introductions and high-capacity diskettes and CD-ROM. It locates and destroys unidentified macro viruses, quarantines suspected or infected files, and will destroy or repair files automatically.
- Symantec Corp.'s popular "Norton AntiVirus" line of products protects computers from viruses, and provides other protections. The latest version, Norton Internet Security 3.0, provides anti-virus, personal firewall and parental controls. The company also sells a stand-alone version of Norton AntiVirus and Norton Personal Firewall. As do other products, it works in the system's background to protect the computer; the newer versions automatically update their virus definitions when the system is connected to the Internet.

- The Free Site.com. This site is one of many on the Internet that offer free anti-virus software utilities. The site offers such products as AntiVir, InoculateIT, MailCleaner, AVG 6.0, Trend Enterprise Solution CD for networks, AnyWare Antivirus, F-PROT, and others. Visit http://www.thefreesite.com/antivirus.htm.
- VBS Defender. This free utility from *PC World* magazine changes VBS File defaults from Open to Edit and protects the system from future VBS file assaults: http://www.pcworld.com/downloads/file_description/0,fid,8106,00.asp
- HushMail (http://www.hushmail.com), Mailsafe (http://www.mailsafe.org), SigabaSecure (http://www.sigabasecure.com) and ZoneAlarm(http://www.zonelabs.com). These applications help secure your email. Depending on the service, they either encrypt your email or to mitigate the threat from destructive content sent embedded in email messages that use HTML (hypertext markup language) to turn email messages into rich media including borders, graphics, images – and possibly destructive or intrusive scripts or applets.

Anti-virus programs should be updated frequently. Some manufacturers recommend weekly downloads of new upgrades designed to catch the latest viruses floating through the Internet. Updating your software can be a simple process; usually at installation, a pop-up window is created to remind the user to update the software and automatically dial into a toll-free number or log on to the manufacturer's Web site to facilitate the upgrade.

FIREWALLS & ANTI-HACKING PROTECTION

Imagine you just got hooked up to that ultra-fast digital subscriber line (DSL) or cable modem service from your local provider. You're thrilled to have the speed of changing television channels

WHAT IF...?

... you received a message from a friend asking you to open an attachment or visit a Web site? Do you open email messages and attachments without pausing to scan the Sender or Subject lines. That's how Anna Kournikova made a name for herself online: the virus tapped people's email programs to disseminate itself. So the message appeared as if it was from a friend or past acquaintance. *Read the Sender and Subject lines* of in-bound email – and consider whether the sender would be likely to distribute such content. Make it a practice to *not* open attachments, unless you're assured the sender would have sent such content, it cannot be sent as a message pasted into an email – and that your anti-virus software is up-to-date. The preview pane function in Microsoft Outlook allows users to preview suspect messages – although it's not a foolproof way to avoid opening and activating all viruses.

---

when you surf the Web – and computer hackers out on the Internet are thrilled that your computer is open for their hacking business 24/7. Broadband connections offer high-speed service – but the pitch neglects to mention one essential warning: You're potentially sharing your computer's hard drive with anyone on the Internet. Because most broadband providers neither warn you about the threat, nor provide the tools to protect your system, maybe it's time you considered a firewall.

With the introduction and growing use of always-on Internet connections, hackers are having an easier time than ever finding their way into people's home-based computers. Unlike traditional dial-up Internet access accounts, which issue a different, dynamic IP address each time the subscriber accesses the Internet, always-on connections use the same connection without ever disconnecting (so long as the computer is left on). Firewalls can help hide the IP address of an individual or each unit on a network station. Although DSL is considered less vulnerable than cable modems, both can give hackers reliable entry into your computer – now and in the future. With cable modems, even consumers on the local system or subnet have access to your system or network.

Once there, they often have free rein over the system – opening files, pirating content, destroying data or leaving behind files or strands of code of their own designed to do anything from slow your computer to distribute a message on the Internet to destroy your computer or network. Whether conducted as a prank or with malicious intent, your vulnerability – and that of everyone on the network you're accessing – exists.

That is, unless you have a firewall. Anti-hacking firewalls hearken an image from their maritime and building-construction etymology: They keep fires (in this case, attacks from the outside) on the other side of the wall, thereby protecting you from attack. Few modem manufacturers and broadband access providers are providing customers with firewalls, nor are they warning customers about firewall installation and use. Few even want to discuss the issue. It's up to you.

Firewall products come in both software and hardware applications. With the growing use of home-based virtual private networks and local area networks that connect multiple computers, it's important to use a product that protects the Internet connection at or near the point of entry into the home. This way, any computers on the network are safe and won't require separate protection.

Two popular software firewall products are McAfee's Firewall and Symantec's Norton Internet Security 2001. Some other products include the Checkpoint Firewall-1 from Sofaware (http://www.sofaware.com), which is being integrated into some cable modems; Sharp Technology Inc.'s Hack Tracer II, which allows users to block hacking attempts and electronically trace hack-

COMPUTER, LAPTOP & DATA SECURITY & PROTECTION

ers on a world map to their starting point – and report the activity to the hacker's Internet Service Provider; and ZoneAlarm, a software-based firewall that includes anti-virus and other features.

Firewall hardware products can support multiple users on a network and provide greater protection against intrusion to a single computer or an entire network. Effective products should include some or all of the following benefits:

- Security for home networks, surpassing that provided by cable/DSL network address translation (NAT) routers.
  Stateful Packet Inspection technology to prevent Denial of Service attacks and malicious data packets, allowing users to share Cable and DSL service safely among all networked computers.
- Real-time email alerts to notify users of hacking attacks or attempts.
- Virtual private network (VPN) pass through.
- Content filtering capabilities that enable parents to monitor and restrict their children's access to objectionable online material, plus logging functions that report user Internet activity and connect times.
- The ability to connect and protect multiple computers.

Some manufacturers include NETGEAR Inc. (www.netgear.com), which released in 2001 its FR314 Cable/DSL Firewall Router, D-Link (http://www.dlink.com), WatchGuard (http://www.watchguard.com), SonicWALL SOHO (http://www.sonicwall.com), and SOHOware's BroadGuard line of secure cable/DSL routers. Visit http://www.firewallguide.com

Other products augment firewall applications. Internet "agents" provide a protective layer to help secure the computer or network. Used in conjunction with a firewall, they can be configured to filter inbound content, and control access to sites or chat rooms based on pre-selected content (such as mention of drugs, sex or other questionable content). Products include Network ICE's BlackICE (http://www.networkice.com) or McAfee's Internet Guard Dog (http://www.mcafee.com).

To ensure your firewall is secure, visit Gibson Research Corp.'s LeakTest (http://grc.com/lt/leaktest.htm) for a free, downloadable security test. This test, part of its ShieldsUp Internet Security Test line of products, will verify that your firewall is operating properly and rebuffing all potential intrusions. The company also has produced "Patchwork," a freeware utility that can instantly determine whether a Windows NT or Windows 2000 operating system server is vulnerable to attacks.

Supplement the system's firewall with firewall log analyzers. These products help users decipher firewall logs, and determine between friendly or malicious entries. Products in this realm include:

- ZoneAlarm's ZoneLog (http://www.zonelog.co.uk).
- BlackICE Defender's free ICEWatch v2.19 (http://keir.net/icewatch.html).

INTRUSION DETECTION SYSTEMS (IDS)

You have your anti-virus, firewall and encryption protection. What about an intrusion detection system? An IDS is similar to a burglar alarm for a computer or network. It monitors traffic on the system and alerts the user or network administrator of any suspicious activity or identification of suspected attack signatures. According to an essay and product review in *Zone Labs Security Update* (www.securityportal.com), this is a complex issue – but one of rising concern, especially among corporations with large networks. Is it of prime concern to home officers? Not yet. But with the advent of always-on connections and the desire of hackers to gain entry, expect to hear more about IDS products in the coming years from such software and security providers as Symantec, Network Security Wizards/Enterasys, Network Ice, Cisco, Network Flight Recorder and Intrusion.com.

WHAT IF...?

... a virus, bug, worm or other malicious product (or malware) reached and corrupted your computer? Would your content be lost and your business irreparably damaged? Purchase, install and use utility programs that help rebuild or restore function to your computer. The products also help clean your hard drive to ensure it's operating efficiently.

SMART PRACTICES & POLICIES

If computer security is a process, here are a few more elements to add to your safety protocol:

- Keep a low profile while online. Whether for fun or to visit with professional peers, if you visit chatrooms or join news groups, know what they're all about first. Chat with some of the users first, or lurk just to take in some of the discussion. Never get into heated "flame wars" with fellow members or visitors; you don't know their intentions or whether they'd retaliate.
- Guard your personal email address. Some Internet service providers (ISP) give out several email addresses as part of a subscriber's account. Create one that will be your private address. Use this one only for personal correspondence with family, friends and business associates. Establish another address for subscriptions, online chat or other public uses. Once released, your private email easily can become part of email lists, resulting in spam and other unwanted mailings.

- Turn off file sharing. Windows 95/98 systems can be configured to share functions (such as printers and devices) as well as files. File Sharing allows others on the network – or, by extension, the Internet – to see, use, copy and alter the contents of your hard drive or other media devices. Even if you only disengage the function when leaving for lunch or an appointment, by turning off File Sharing, you're closing a significant potential security breach.
- Protect your PIM. In some computers, personally identifiable information (PIM), such as a user's name, address and phone number, is embedded in the computer's processor. It even collects software preferences and tracks Web surfing habits. These cookies are a marketer's bonanza – and a bane to personal privacy.
- Survey your system safety tools. Conduct a vulnerability survey. Such products as intrusion detector BlackIce Defender (www.networkice.com); port vulnerability scanner Shields Up (www.grc.com); Symantec's Norton Internet Security 2000 (which combines anti-virus and personal firewall protection); and firewall and anti-virus provider Zone Labs (www.zonelabs.com) can create a web of anti-virus and hacking protection.
- Log off. When not using your computer or Internet connection, log off from your ISP. Logging back on usually takes less than a minute, and by disconnecting from the Net you're eliminating any chance that a hacker will find you during that session.
- Push for heightened security measures from your broadband provider. The need for security eventually will become a unique selling point for the more successful DSL and cable modem providers. Until then, we can only demand it – and hope it will come.

COMPUTER, LAPTOP & DATA SECURITY & PROTECTION

DATA BACKUP

When was the last time you backed up your computer data? Yesterday? Last week? This year? Fewer than four percent of computer users admit to regularly backing up their computer content. Hence, a computer backup regimen is an often neglected element of working in the information age. But imagine if a lightning strike blew your hard drive, or a virus corrupted your data files, or a thief made off with your entire computer. All that data – lost forever – unless you have a tape or diskette copy in your safe or at a neighbor's house.

How often you back up your computer depends on how often and how much new content is being input into the machine. If you only occasionally use the computer for client correspondence, then a weekly or biweekly backup could be sufficient. If you crank out six hours of computer-intensive work each day, you likely should be backing up at day's end. The essential element to data backup is never to be in a position where you could lose irreplaceable content.

Do you own and use a computer backup device or application? You can copy single files to a 3.5-inch floppy diskette, or copy entire directories to a ZIP disk or tape backup. Most important is to have a system for backing up your content. It won't happen on its own. Any backup regimen should be:

- Secure. It must provide secure and safe storage for any critical or "can't afford to lose" data. It's not just the backup process; it's where you put the media with the data.
- Frequent. It must be performed frequently enough to keep up with any changes made to the data.
- Simple to do. If it's not a simple process, it won't get done.
- Easy to restore. If your system went down, your stored content must be easy to restore or retrieve.

Which system you use to store your data depends on the volume of data you have. If you infrequently use the computer, backing up to a 3.5-inch floppy is as simple as slipping a diskette into the drive, going into Windows Explorer, and dragging the selected files to the floppy drive icon. If you're backing up directories of individual files, such as word processing documents, a ZIP drive or large-capacity diskette could provide ample storage capacity. If you work with volumes of large files, a tape drive likely will handle most of your content. Here are the benefits of each:

- Diskette drive: Whether copying files for travel or saving documents for safekeeping the diskette drive is the simplest solution. At 1.44 megabytes each, these 3.5-inch diskettes also have the most limited volume of any of the options available. Even using compression technology, as your needs for larger capacity grow, you likely will want to move to a larger-volume system.
- High-capacity, magnetic cartridge drives: The ZIP disk from Iomega Corporation, and others like it provide high-capacity storage and retrieval systems, ranging from 100 megabytes to more than 250MB – and more when compressed. After the initial install and backup session, subsequent backups are conducted in a one-step process. One caveat: It's often difficult to retrieve single files if multiple folders were stored in a scheduled backup.
- CDRW: Writeable CD-ROMs have become a simple way to copy and save content to a media product. And with the ubiquity of the CD-ROM and CDRW drive in desktop and laptop computers, any data saved can be transported easily, viewed or retrieved from another system with a CD-ROM drive.
- Tape drives: A tape drive is an external system of copying or retrieving larger amounts of content. Easy to use and economical, the quarter-inch cartridge (QIC) format provides capacity ranging from 20MB to four gigabytes (GB) of uncompressed data. Even minitapes, which are used frequently in PCs, have capacity exceeding 680MB. Unlike

the other media mentioned, tape drives, including QIC and digital audio tape (DAT) can only access data sequentially as it was saved to the device; you can't skip ahead to a file or document.

- Online backup services: With an online backup service, the computer user accesses a Web-based service provider to backup any or all of a computer's hard drive. The user selects the content to be backed up, and then executes the upload. Content is stored and accessible remotely on the provider's Web server. Providers include ManagedStorage.com's PowerBAK Personal Edition ($5.95 a month for 100 megabytes of storage), and @Backup (www.@backup.com, $99 a year for 100 megabytes).

Backup doesn't happen in a vacuum. More than just owning the hardware and software, you also need to create a system for your backup process. In your datebook or contact management or calendar software, insert a regular reminder or tickler to remind you to conduct a content backup.

NOTES:

NOTES:

CHAPTER VI
PROTECTING YOURSELF OUTSIDE THE HOME OFFICE

Chapter Overview: With a laptop computer, critical files, even your wallet and cash, you're an even more vulnerable target outside the home office than inside. This chapter will delve into smart practices that will keep the home officer and teleworker safe while on the road or working outside the home office.

So now your home office may resemble Fort Knox. It has been fortified from the outside, and protection of your computer, files, media storage and other elements has been addressed.

What about your life on the road? Whether you're on appointments around town or traveling to another city, develop street smarts about how you conduct yourself on the road. This book has used the "What if ...?" concept as an editorial element addressing security in and around the home and home office, but the streets also are an important place for the device.

The best advice remains: Stay alert at all times. Be keen to stalkers or people following you. Above all: Trust your gut instincts.

VEHICLE & PERSONAL SAFETY

When walking down a city street, or heading from the parking lot and into an office building, if possible avoid walking alone, and steer clear of shortcuts or deserted areas. Stay near groups or crowds. Walk confidently and with purpose. If you make eye contact as you

PROTECTING YOURSELF OUTSIDE THE HOME OFFICE

approach or pass others, stand tall and exude fortitude in your presence. Women should avoid wearing jewelry. Instead of carrying a loose purse, wear it with the strap across the chest and beneath a jacket, or carry it under your arm. If a thief tries to snatch your purse, briefcase or attache, don't resist.

Avoid carrying large amounts of cash. If you must, before leaving the privacy of your home office, corporate office, car or hotel room, separate out enough cash for miscellaneous expenses and carry that in your pocket, wallet or purse. Use a money belt or other device hidden beneath your clothing to safely stash the remainder of your cash.

Documents, files or other business-related items should not be left in plain view in the car. They could invite a break-in by a curious thief. Instead, place such items completely under the seat or in the trunk. A briefcase and laptop carry case should not be left in the car during meetings or overnight at a hotel. If the car is stolen, the briefcase or computer will be, too.

If parking in a garage or open lot, park as close to the building or facility entrance as possible. If you expect to return to your vehicle in the evening, park near or beneath a streetlight or other lighting source. Avoid parking beside or near vans, trucks or other large vehicles. Before leaving the building to return to your vehicle, fetch your key ring from your pocket, purse or briefcase. Find your car key, and have it ready for when you approach your car. As an additional safety effort, in case you're attacked, gripping a single key between the index and middle finger – and then forming a fist tightly around the rest of the keys – can provide a painful weapon against an assailant.

Before entering a car, check the back seat and floorboards for anyone who may be hiding. Once in the car, immediately lock the doors, and keep windows closed until the car is moving. Keep your purse, briefcase, attache or laptop case on the passenger-side floor or under the seat where possible.

Once in a building, peer into elevators before entering. If you will be entering the elevator with another individual, or if one person already is inside, and you are suspicious of the person, wait for the next elevator. Once inside, stand beside the control panel and scan it for the emergency call button. Determine, for example, whether the emergency button must be pushed or pulled. Is there an emergency phone? How does the box open (a turn knob, lever or other mechanism)?

VEHICLE SAFETY KIT

Depending on where you live, you should have several safety and security items always stored inside your vehicle. These include:

- Flashlight.
- First aid kit (see Chapter II for contents).
- Flares and reflectors.
- Center punch or small hammer, used to break a window in case the car runs into a lake, canal or other deep body of water.
- T-shaped lug wrench to provide leverage in removing lug nuts from the wheel and facilitate changing a tire.
- Blizzard survival kit: a blanket, canned or packaged non-perishable food and water boxed and stored in the trunk.

PREPARING FOR TRAVEL

Traveling on business or pleasure presents a unique challenge to the home office worker. Before leaving on vacation, prepare the office for your time away. When traveling for a few days or longer, back up important data files to diskette or RWCD-ROM, and store those diskettes in the safe, a neighbor's home or the safe-deposit box.

PROTECTING YOURSELF OUTSIDE THE HOME OFFICE

Then treat the home office like the home. Clean up the office and workspace, and close the office blinds. Some travelers prefer to leave a few home blinds open to give the appearance that the home is not closed up. Turn on a few lights; put others on automatic timers. Turn down the ringers on the phones – or turn the answering machines or voicemail systems to answer phones on the first ring – so the incessant ring doesn't make the home sound vacant. Lock all the windows and doors to the outside, and lock the door from the office to the house. Turn off the automatic garage door opener. Lock the door leading from the garage into the home.

Another option for managing in-bound telephone calls is to use call forwarding to transfer incoming calls to an associate or employee who can take messages or handle some client requests. This will help maintain the business activity while you're away, and give the business an appearance of being staffed – even when you're not available. You also can give that ally your voicemail access code so he or she can retrieve any messages and respond appropriately to important calls.

Before departing, arrange to have the newspaper and mail held by the respective service. Or have it picked up and held by a neighbor. Often, home business owners come home to so much business correspondence that being able to pick it up from a friend's home the day of your return means you can go through it before business starts anew on the next day. Knowing that much of the first day back will be spent returning phone messages and catching up with clients, co-workers and peers, getting the mail out of the way early can heighten productivity.

When you are traveling, you have to balance clients' needs to know you're away with the chance that others will learn that your home and home office are vacant. Determine the primary customers, clients, vendors, co-workers and managers who need to know you'll be away. If appropriate or necessary, provide a back-up contact – perhaps a strategic partner or ally you've worked with in the past. Then, give that backup your contact information in case of

> **WHAT IF…?**
>
> … you found yourself on a busy street surrounded by people you didn't know? When you're on the road, do you act and dress like a tourist, or do you act like you belong?
>
> The savvy traveler never will appear out of place in any environment or location. Blend in with the locals – and minimize chances of a mugging or other assault. Whether traveling or at home, stay alert. Be aware to what's going on around you.

an emergency. If you've ever reached the voicemail of a corporate contact who was on vacation, he or she might have recorded a greeting telling callers that they're out of the office for a few days. How does a home officer do that – without alerting the world that there's no one around to watch the space? The outgoing greeting could say:

"You've reached 555-1234. We will be unavailable the week of _____. Please leave a message and we will return the call at our earliest convenience. If you need assistance right away, contact _____."

This message doesn't say you're away; it says you're unavailable. It provides the duration of the closure, so people have an expectation of how long before you'll likely be calling back. And it provides a contact in case of an emergency. Just because you run a home-based enterprise doesn't mean you want to lose business or leave clients feeling they're without recourse if they need help with a project.

Before leaving, alert the police to your travel plans, and ask for increased patrols in your neighborhood to ensure a heightened presence while you're away. Have a neighbor park his or her car in your driveway; alert the police that a car might be in the driveway. Leave travel contact information with family, a neighbor and your business allies or a co-worker.

> ### WEB TRAVEL RESOURCES
>
> The Web is a traveler's friend. Planning a trip to a destination you've never visited before? Want to get a heads-up on safety issues there? Hit iTravelSafe.com, a Web site that provides travel safety information, advisories and tips to subscribers via daily email. The news is compiled from more than 5,000 independent sources and governments. The company also has a security registry for members to register trip plans and emergency contacts online.
>
> If you're away and wondering whether any bad weather is threatening your hometown, hit http://208.184.24.125/. The Emergency Email Network will alert users when a natural disaster strikes in their area, whether it's a tsunami in Hawaii or a hurricane along the Atlantic coast.

Several tools can help secure a hotel room when on the road. A small, rubber door stopper purchased at a discount or home-improvement store can be wedged between the door and the threshold. This will help prevent forced entry into the room at night after you have retired for the evening. For added security, portable door alarms designed to hang from the door handle will emit an audible alarm if the door is opened. They can be set off by motion or wiggling of the handle, or if a wire is separated from a metal contact when the door is opened. Both tools are small and light-weight enough to be carried easily by the traveler.

PROTECTING YOUR LAPTOP

Your laptop might be your remote office power tool. But is it a thief-magnet as well? Each year, more than $1 billion a year in desktop and laptop computer hardware is lost. That amounts to an estimated $15 billion annually in intellectual property and data lost, according to CompuTrace, a manufacturer of theft-detection software.

About 400 of the more than 1,000 laptop computers stolen daily are taken from office locations, leaving the remainder vulnerable in cars, airports and other public locations, according to Safeware Insurance (www.safeware.com), the Columbus, Ohio-based computer insurance company. Protect computer hardware before it's lifted from the premises or car.

Avoiding laptop theft is part device or tool, and part behavior. Whether they use their laptops for business or pleasure while traveling, owners can protect their equipment by:

- Being alert. When traveling or carrying your laptop outside the home office, keep it close at hand and be aware of your surroundings.
- Using the right tools. As with home office safety, protecting the laptop calls for a layering effect of several anti-theft devices designed to decrease the likelihood that the unit could be stolen.
- Staying up-to-date. As new tools are developed, upgrade the theft-prevention devices to make it more difficult for someone to steal the computer.

Laptop owners can reduce the attraction and thwart theft with cable locks, audible alarms, passwords and even biometrics that allow only the owner to access and use the unit.

Kryptonite's cable locks and KryptoVault lock (www.kryptonitelock.com) help secure the laptop to a desktop or other secure object. The company also has motion sensor alarms that emit a loud sound

PROTECTING YOURSELF OUTSIDE THE HOME OFFICE

if the laptop is moved. Low-tech tools include key locks, such as Secure-It Inc.'s X-Lock cable ($29.95), the Universal Adhesive Lock that tethers the unit to a desk with permanent adhesive ($39.95), The Notepad secures the laptop beneath a crossbar cabled to the workstation ($79.95); or the Vanguard II attaches to the 9-pin adapter on the back of the PC ($39.95). As with most cable lock products, Kensington locks (www.kensington.com) fit within the Kensington Security Slot in the back of many brands of laptops. The MicroSaver's six-foot steel cable can then be wrapped around any immovable object. Use of a Kensington slot cable locking device is not intended to be failsafe, but it can deter novice thieves or opportunists who might otherwise take an unsecured laptop.

The Targus (www.targus.com) DEFCON 1 Notebook Computer Security System ($46.95) combines a stainless steel cable and motion sensor that transmits a 45-second 110 dB audible alarm whenever the cable is severed or the unit is moved. An indicator light warns thieves that the device is armed. Trackit (www.trackit-corp.com) uses a keychain transmitter and a miniature receiver to let the laptop owner monitor the computer – or a briefcase, purse, carry-on luggage or any bag – up to 40 feet away. If the owner gets separated from the computer or case, a 110-decible siren sounds.

Computrace 8.0 from Absolute Software (www.absolute.com) is like Lo-Jack for computers. Similar to CyberAngel, once loaded onto a hard drive, the system sends a silent message over phone lines or the Internet to Absolute's offices. If the owner reports the unit stolen, Absolute can trace the source's phone number or IP address. Once located, Computrace alerts the police or corporate security to retrieve the unit. Call-blocking features can't hide its whereabouts in North America, and hard drive reformatting and disk partitioning won't erase the hidden software. Prices start at $49.95 for an annual agreement for a single PC, which includes software, monitoring and recovery services. The system works with any Windows-based system; it is not Macintosh compatible.

Caveo Technology's Caveo Anti-Theft (www.caveo.com) is a combination software-hardware device that creates a unique form of biometric security. A tilt-motion sensor is installed on a PC card or motherboard, and the software application disables the laptop if it is stolen. The owner or user creates a physical "motion password" that consists of two or more angled or tilting motions of the computer. The motion is designed to engage or disengage the software alarm, creating "location awareness" in the computer; in essence, it knows when it should be stationary. Once the system is engaged, the motion of someone lifting or walking with the laptop – but not idle bumping or brushing against it – will set off the alarm. The system also locks down access to data so outsiders cannot review or download content from the computer.

Using a hybrid proximity and motion detector, the Lexent (www.lexent.com) iSpy with PC Radar ($147.95) is a laptop theft prevention device, which not only uses motion, but determines whether the motion is likely to be mal-intentioned. It also alerts the owner to this motion with a two-way communication via a fob-like device. Depending on the combination of motion and fob (owner) proximity, the unit will decide whether to alert the home owner by way of a piercing siren. If the fob and laptop are separated, the unit will sense the separation and automatically arm itself. Once armed, if the separation increases to a preset distance (100 feet is recommended) the device will either alert the fob holder, or set off the alarm. Using the fob device, the owner also can set off the alarm remotely. The company recommends the iSpy be used in conjunction with a security cable to create a powerful and effective anti-theft tool.

Although most computer manufacturers rely on after-market products to secure their laptops, IBM's Smartcard Security Kit ($199) uses a PCMCIA card with a smart card that's inserted to ensure only the owner has access. The kit works on all but three laptop brands. IBM's Asset ID Technology for several of its ThinkPad laptop computers uses a radio frequency transmitter installed in the laptop. This can be configured with a company's security system to set off an alarm or video camera – like an inventory control system.

PROTECTING YOURSELF OUTSIDE THE HOME OFFICE

Still, the most effective laptop asset protection starts with the owner:

- Engrave or write with permanent market your name and driver license number (including the two-letter state code) onto the hardware. If the computer is company owned, discuss the appropriate asset-tagging device with the information technology department.
- Write the serial number in documents you travel with. Also, write the serial number on a photograph of the unit and store that in the safe at the home office.
- Regularly backup data, especially when traveling, and carry the diskette separately from the computer.
- Frequently change your access password.
- When traveling, use a nondescript attache to carry the laptop, instead of a laptop carrying case.
- Keep the unit close at hand, especially in public, while manning a trade show booth, while traveling or while passing through airport security checkpoints. Be suspicious of people or events that could be deliberate attempts to distract you so someone can steal the unit.
- If you have to leave your laptop in the car, place it in the trunk – *before* you arrive at your destination, not once you get there.
- Boost your insurance if necessary. A laptop stolen from the home office or while traveling may not be covered by standard homeowners insurance. Talk with your agent to determine whether your home-business or residential coverage extends to your laptop, or if you should purchase additional coverage or a rider to protect the unit.

NOTES:

PROTECTING YOURSELF OUTSIDE THE HOME OFFICE

NOTES:

CHAPTER VIII
WORKSPACE SAFETY & OSHA ISSUES

Chapter Overview: Ergonomics and workplace design isn't just for corporate offices. Savvy home officers implement the latest workplace design thinking to stave off repetitive-motion induced injuries, undue stresses on the body and mind, and to create a more comfortable, safe and inviting home office.

In 2000, the U.S. Occupational Safety & Health Administration attempted to apply traditional office- and workplace-related safety guidelines to the home offices of corporate teleworkers. The issue created a firestorm of debate about the federal government's role in regulating the home-based workplace – a debate and discussion that didn't die with OSHA's withdrawal of its letter of interpretation just days later.

The idea is not without merit: No matter the location or ownership of the workplace, workers and their employers should strive to create a safe and healthy work environment for all workers. This includes teleworkers and entrepreneurs working from home.

The overriding principle here is to make your workplace safe and comfortable. When surveying your home office and its environs, from the curb to your office itself, is it a safe place to work or visit? Are paver bricks or stepping stones sticking up and likely to cause someone to trip or fall (a mantra in the personal-injury law business). Is your dog aggressive? Should it be closed in a bedroom when customers or clients arrive? Is your chair an aged relic with loose

WORKSPACE SAFETY & OSHA ISSUES

mechanisms that could result in its toppling over and injuring you or another user?

Is the home office a place for OSHA compliance? Although the home officer may not have to report the workspace's safety compliance record to the federal government, it's a wise investment in time and organizational strategy to ensure the space is comfortable and safe.

How safe is your home office? Have you conducted a safety survey of the worksite lately? Use this home office safety checklist to help ensure the workplace is a safe place:

- Ditch the clutter. Loose newspapers and magazines left haphazardly around the office floor can become a slip-and-fall accident waiting to happen – to you, your family or business associates or clients. Create a place for your periodicals, both current and older ones. This way, they'll be accessible from a safe place.
- Does the home office engage in safe electrical usage, with reasonable use of extension cords and power strips, wire chases or limited exposed wiring to help prevent children or pets from getting tangled or shocked? Outlets and power-strips should not be overburdened with appliances. Instead, use other outlets in order to minimize the potential for shock or fire hazard.
- Where are the electrical outlets and phone jacks in relation to the desk? Will children in the home find enjoyment playing with an entangled morass of cables and wires, or would the desk best be perched in front of any outlets or jacks? Wires dangling along a baseboard also are visually unappealing.
- Purchase and keep nearby a fully-charged fire extinguisher (often required as part of a city or county occupational license), a complete first-aid kit, escape ladders where needed, and a list of emergency medical contacts.

- Use only the latest ergonomic furnishings, from adjustable chairs to desks suited to the individual worker to telephone headsets.
- If you telework, review your home office setup and updated safety regimen with your employer. If you manage a telework program, address these issues to ensure your employees are working from a safe workplace. Make this a required part of the company's signed telework policy and agreement.
- Create an OSHA-compliant workplace. Although your home office doesn't have to meet the strict federal guidelines the traditional office does, making sure yours meets basic safety practices and levels can help avoid accidents.

WHAT IF...?

... employees balk about ensuring their home-based workplace is safety-compliant? What can an employer do to make sure the company isn't responsible or liable in case of injury? Link telework opportunities to home office safety. Require the employee to provide photographs of the home office (plus the home's approach, if clients or other workers ever are to visit) and a signed affidavit that the workplace meets minimum safety standards. Telework is an employee privilege, not the requirement of an employer. And the employer should not assume heightened responsibility from the alternative work arrangement.

ERGONOMICS BLEND MIND & BODY IN WORKPLACE FUNCTION

A funny thing happened on the way to the modern office. People forgot how to use their bodies correctly. They'll sit like statues for hours on end, taking no breaks other than to hit the bathroom or kitchen. And stretching the body? That's for the gym - a costly facility whose membership they haven't used in months because they've been working too much.

Do your wrists and hands ache from excessive typing? Are your neck and shoulders sore from having a telephone receiver wedged between them? Does the old kitchen or folding chair you requisitioned for your home office leaving you with a pain in the back, legs and shoulders?

This is not good. Talk to almost any certified professional ergonomist and central to his or her mantra is a training program designed to create a smarter worker. And a smarter worker, they surmise, is a healthier – and less expensive – worker. From at-home worker to road warrior, ergonomics – the science of "human factors engineering," which matches workplace to worker – has its place in every worker's business environment.

Think about the graphic designer who works the mouse like a maven – but never breaks to stretch the wrists. Or consider the keyboard junkie who easily taps out 10,000 key strokes an hour. Without stretching the arms, wrists and hands, legs, back or neck, his muscles will teem with stress.

Ergonomics and stretching seek to increase productivity and promote overall worker health and satisfaction by minimizing discomfort and cumulative workplace injuries. These repetitive stress injuries (RSI), such as carpal tunnel syndrome and tendinitis, cost American companies almost $20 billion a year in lost time and insurance benefits paid. In fact, ergonomic ailments are considered among the fastest-growing work-related illnesses, accounting for almost a third of workplace maladies reported to OSHA. So if you're stymied by sore shoulders, an aching back, a stiff or painful neck, and pains in your wrists, head or eyes, ergonomic intervention could be your remedy. RSIs are caused by incorrect posture and poorly designed workspaces. Often they can be remedied by implementing better workplace design, and even purchasing and using the right furniture and accessories to encourage proper seating, posture and use of tools.

What's the first step to creating an ergonomically-inviting workplace? Learn and implement. Study your workplace and your work habits, and figure out if the two jibe, keeping in mind the three rules of anthropometry, or human factors engineering and workstation design:

1. Where possible, make furniture and workstations adjustable.
2. Design clearances – like kneeholes beneath desks or the distance to the wall – to accommodate 95 percent of all men.
3. Design reach distances to accommodate 95 percent of all women.

An ergonomic makeover doesn't have to be expensive to be effective. Some estimate that about 20 percent of all ergonomic changes cost nothing to implement. Whether you buy your furnishings from a store or make them yourself with supplies found around the home, the goal is the create a comfortable workplace. Here are some ways to implement your own ergonomic solution:

- Chairs: Look for ergonomically-designed chairs with adjustable armrests, seats and backs to ease stress on the arms, shoulders and backs. A quality ergonomic chair can range from $100 to more than $1,000. If you buy a new chair, read the instructions to use the different levers and adjustments. If you want to improve your existing chair, using a rolled-up tower or small in-flight pillow placed behind the lower back can help support the lumbar region.

WORKSPACE SAFETY & OSHA ISSUES

- Footrests: Use a footrest to raise and comfort legs and take weight off the lower back. A store-bought foot rest can cost from $40 to $80. Some have rubber stubs that massage the soles of the feet. For a free alternative, create a footrest by stacking one or two telephone books, taping them together or wrapping them in a mailing pouch, and placing beneath the feet.

- Computer keyboards, wrist rests and mouse pads: Ergonomic computer keyboards angle a typist's hands toward each other in a more natural alignment. Wrist rests and mouse pads - or left-handed mice for southpaws - help ease lower arm pain. If necessary, use an articulating keyboard tray to raise or lower, tilt, or push outward the keyboard to accommodate the user.

- Telephone headsets: Not only do headsets reduce neck strain, they ease functionality of the workspace by removing several steps from answering and dialing the telephone. Instead of reaching for the receiver and thrusting it between your head and shoulder, you instead only push a button or lift the receiver off the telephone cradle (depending on the phone). Price: from $20 to more than $100.

The creation of a home office ergonomic program requires a review of how you work. Implement these ideas in any home office setting, and physical conditions and productivity could improve:

- Sit well: Always adjust chairs after sitting. Readjust your own chair daily. Try to attain a neutral posture, with 90-degree angles in the elbows and knees. Buy chairs with armrests, five legs on casters for wide support, and which promote a natural, "lazy S" curve in the back. Seat height should rise to within 10 inches from the bottom side of the desk. The desk or any fixed-height work surface should be 30 inches (give or take, depending upon user). From the floor to the bottom of the work surface should be 26 inches. Depth (from body part to wall) should be at least 15 inches at the knee and 26 inches at the feet. Under-table width should be at least 20 inches to provide side motion.

- Don't lean: Phones, pens and other common items should be between 15 and 30 inches from the seated worker. The writing area should be at a 45-degree angle to the writing side of the computer station.
- See it clearly: Computer monitors should be positioned 18 and 30 inches from the eyes, and from seven and 15 degrees below eye level. Dust the monitor and desktop frequently to create a better view and reduce allergens. Change air filters in the home monthly.
- Position a document holder at roughly the same distance and height as the computer monitor. This will help eliminate neck pains from viewing papers laid flat upon the desk, and eye strain from having to refocus.
- Cut the glare: If light from windows casts a glare on computer monitors, install shades – and use them. If lamps or overhead lights create glare, change the angle of the light or monitor. Still, at cooler moments of the day, take advantage of open shades to bathe the office in natural light. Full-spectrum lighting overhead casts a soothing, sun-like glow on the entire workplace.
- Frequently change your posture: Shift the legs, arms and back to help break up the accumulation of lactic acid that can cause muscle pain.
- Stretch that body: While seated, interlock the fingers and stretch the arms skyward. Let go, and repeat behind the back, straightening the arms. Rotate your waist in your seat, stretch the neck in all directions, arch the back – always trying to gently loosen your joints, flex your muscles and ultimately attain full range of motion. Typists should stretch the fingers and arms. With one arm outstretched and the palm up, gently pull downward on the fingers with

WORKSPACE SAFETY & OSHA ISSUES

the other hand. Then pull the thumb back toward the wrist. Switch hands and repeat.
- Change your view: Frequently look away from the monitor or desktop. Refocus on a distant object. This will help eliminate or reduce the likelihood of headaches caused by staring at a computer monitor for long periods.
- Take a break: Occasionally get up from the desk and walk around. This can loosen the muscles and recharge the mind.
- Think healthy: In any work setting, having the right mindset is essential to feeling good. Survey your surroundings to identify any area that could be improved to deliver more comfort, whether emotional or physical. Such improvements could include the chair, computer and desk, or putting pictures and personal items around the office to enliven it and boost your emotions while there.

STRESS MANAGEMENT

Ever get stressed – even when you're working from home? With the deluge of information, time demands and other stresses placed on the 21st century worker's life, stress is part of the everyday experience – even for the home officer.

Men and women executives are striving to deliver more. Dual-income families are faced with tight deadlines and tighter employer and client expectations. As entrepreneurs in home offices, we are the top managers – and bear the burdens of the title. We're pushing ourselves to achieve, excel and produce more than ever before.

Stress leads to tension and conflict. Workers become at odds with themselves, their clients and their families. At some point, something has got to give – unless we hit the check valve and release some of the pressure. Stress can lead to loss of concentration, short-tempered reactions to family and client issues, and even hysteria. Stress also can develop into such medical problems as headaches, exhaustion, ulcers and sick days – even for the home officer.

Stress management requires identifying and remedying the cause, and simultaneously reducing the symptoms. This way, we can reduce the stress we face during the workday – and the symptoms that slide into our private lives. Try to implement these tips to help reduce or eliminate the stress that causes tension and conflict in your work and personal life:

- Don't over-schedule. Manage your time better. Resolve scheduling conflicts by agreeing to take on only what you can reasonably accomplish. Overworking is common to at-home workers. Allowing long hours to become a regimen of all-nighters can lead to increased stress and the resulting maladies.
- Improve your relations. Whether they are peer or colleague relations, clients and customers, business partners, suppliers and vendors, or family members, eliminate or resolve conflicts promptly and seek closure to vexing issues or debates.
- Decrease dissension among family members, and seek acceptance and understanding of the home-based workspace.
- Take mental health days. Taking time off for yourself is important. If doing so won't conflict with deadlines, take a day off, or schedule a long weekend away – even if it's at a nearby vacation getaway.
- Meditate, massage and exercise. Whether you're sitting upright on the floor in the lotus position breathing deeply, treating yourself to a massage, walking around the neighborhood, or riding the stationary cycle at the gym, make and take time for yourself. Set aside time each day to meditate, exercise, or just walk or relax. Devoting time to your mental and physical self can cleanse your mind and improve your dedication and productivity.
- Eliminate clutter. A clean workplace can help you achieve efficiency, improve output and gain control over your work

WORKSPACE SAFETY & OSHA ISSUES

life. Whether it's a new file cabinet, a redesigned closet to accommodate your files and supplies, or a new desk to provide a larger workspace, cleaning your environment can help your business.

- Create an inviting workplace. Whether it's wind chimes outside your office window, or your favorite CD spinning on the office stereo or the computer's multimedia player, the more at home you feel in your home office the more at ease your mind will feel while in that space. Consider painting your office in your favorite colors or hues, accentuating it with knicknacks or your life's mementos. Bring in plants, a fish or other pet, space lighting – anything that will make the space yours, and a place you want to be.

- Be happy in your work. Job satisfaction is an important element of good health, and just because you work from home doesn't mean you've made nirvana. Take time to assess what you're doing – and whether you are satisfied. If not, explore ways to broaden – or change – your horizons.

- Maintain a positive mental attitude. Your PMA can immeasurably prevent tension, frayed nerves and a feeling of loss of control.

NOTES:

WORKSPACE SAFETY & OSHA ISSUES

NOTES:

APPENDIX

THE HOME OFFICER'S SAFETY & SECURITY CHECKLIST

- Thorny foliage to protect ground-floor windows to your home – without providing a hiding place for prowlers. Outdoor lighting to illuminate the property at night.

- Window shades or blinds to hide the home office from view so people cannot see the computer, fax machine or other expensive – and enticing – electronic equipment from the road or the home's approach.

- A fireproof safe and/or locking filing cabinet to store and protect important documents and backed-up computer data.

- Ample homeowner and liability insurance to cover business use of technology and other belongings.

- Flashlight. Select a small but powerful penlight for easy storage, or a larger model that will project a bright and wide beam to illuminate a large area. Make sure the batteries are fresh to ensure the flashlight is ready when you need it. Place several flashlights throughout the home, including the office, the bedside table and the kitchen.

- Portable phone. A cordless phone will provide mobility if you need to leave your home office to investigate a noise or if you feel threatened.

- Cellular phone. If someone were attempting to break into your home, he or she could cut your phone lines to keep you or your alarm system from calling out for help. Having your cellular phone charged and on hand provides a reliable lifeline to the world outside. (Helpful hint: Even if your

WORKSPACE SAFETY & OSHA ISSUES

cellular phone is kept in the car or shared by someone else in your home, if you have an older model cell phone lying around, it could help. Many phones, when charged, can be used to dial 911 – even if they don't have service on the unit).

- Personal audible alarm. When activated, these once-popular handheld alarms emit a loud, siren-type noise.

- Mace. Whether you prefer the Mace® brand self-defense spray, or a mustard, pepper or other handheld defense spray, keeping a bottle near your workstation can provide quick defense against an intruder, or an attacking dog if you're outside. Just beware of keeping these and any defense products where children can reach and activate them.

- A fire escape or rope ladder for offices or rooms on second floor.

- Fire extinguisher. These are important for any home – and home office. Even if you have one or several elsewhere in the home, having one in the home office can help you quickly extinguish any electrical or other fire that may break out in or around the office.

- First aid kit. This should include adhesive bandages, alcohol swabs/antiseptic wipes, Neosporin ointment, surgical dressings, gauze rolls, elastic bandages, surgical gloves, and a bottle of syrup of Ipecac. Because this kit likely will be used by other household members, inspect it frequently to ensure it remains well-stocked.

- A safety and security audit was conducted recently of the home office to ensure vulnerability is kept to a minimum.

ADDITIONAL RESOURCES

For more information on home and home office safety and protection, see:

- Institute for Business & Home Safety (www.ibhs.org)
- Insurance Institute for Property Loss Reduction (617-722-0200)
- American Red Cross (www.crossnet.org)
- Federal Emergency Management Agency (FEMA) (www.fema.gov)
- National Safety Council (www.nsc.org)
- The Privacy Rights Clearinghouse (www.privacyrights.org)
- The Identity Theft Survival Kit (www.identitytheft.org) or call 800-725-0807.

SOHO SNAPSHOT:
HOME OFFICE EXUDES SAFETY

Jane Scheid's home office and surrounding property provide plenty of protection – and peace of mind.

If the entry gate to her property doesn't dissuade unwelcome guests, then the alarm company's warning sign might. Lush foliage obstructs the glimpse of casual passersby, while allowing Scheid a clear view outside. At night, motion detectors guarantee that, if someone creeps through the yard, the entire property and her office/cottage will be flooded in bright light.

When she's out of the office, Scheid draws the window blinds so people can't peer in at her equipment. When she's in the office, the deadbolt is often turned, and her cellular phone and a can of Mace are always close at hand.

She is running her marketing communications company alone from her home, yet Scheid rarely feels unsafe. "Maybe I'm just a paranoid person," Scheid says, "bt I take these precautions, and I haven't had anything alarming happen to me yet."

Scheid isn't paranoid – just smart.

SOHO SNAPSHOT:
STEALTH & CUNNING CONCEAL HOME OFFICER

The first sign that greets visitors and passersby to Michael Dziak's Georgia home office is from his alarm company. Other than that, you get little outward indication that the president of InteliWorks Inc. (www.inteliworks.com), a telework consultancy, works from home.

Dziak prefers it that way. In fact, first impressions go a long way toward securing his home office, Dziak says. If people are able to look through the lush, thorny holly bushes that grow outside his ground-floor windows, which themselves are locked, they will see that Dziak has removed the cover to one of his computers (you can't resell a computer without the shell, he surmises). They'll also note that his 17-inch monitor has a sign, boasting: "Monitor defective."

"I operate on a stealth basis," said Dziak, whose neighbors don't even know he works from home. "Even though I'm home all the time, there's no obvious indication that I'm home or not."

Computer data are backed up daily between his desktop computers and his laptop, and a tape backup is performed monthly – and then stored in a remote location of the home, he says. Computers can be replaced in hours. But nine years' worth of data are priceless, he admits.

"It's a lot easier to prevent theft than to try to recover after it's occurred," he says. "It's my contention that the possibility is always there … and everyone should have a contingency plan in place."

SOHO SNAPSHOT:
ONE SAFETY-CONSCIOUS WOMAN

Between the yard and the windows of Carmen Hiers' home is a thick hedge along the entire perimeter of the structure. Others plant thorny vines or plants beneath windows to prevent access from outside.

Although the hedge helps keep the uninvited away, truth be told, Hiers rarely invites anyone to her home office. Instead, the marketing specialist prefers a more safe plan to work with clients: the offices of her corporate clients.

Hiers has an account at a local MailBoxes Etc. She receives almost all mail and parcels there, and this postal company address replaces her home address on all letterhead. Even with new U.S. Postal Service regulations requiring PMB (for "private mail box") be used to denote use of a private facility, Hiers will continue to use her postal box.

Her defense mechanisms serve multiple goals. "I've always made it a practice not to meet clients at home – not only because people tend not to take you as seriously, but also to avoid any complications associated with having people I don't know very well know I live by myself," she said. "As it is, I don't feel comfortable having delivery people figure out that I'm a female living alone."

SOHO SNAPSHOT:
KEEPING A LID ON HER HOME OFFICE ADDRESS

Linda Greck chose another route for her mailing address. Instead of redirecting her mail to a local mailing service, Greck instead put "Suite 100" on stationary for MediaMatters, her public relations firm. Greck wasn't so concerned about hiding her residence as she was presenting a professional image for her limited client base.

It's just another insurance policy, like the business rider Greck added to her homeowner policy to cover her home office equipment

WORKSPACE SAFETY & OSHA ISSUES

– items she says typically are not covered by a traditional homeowner or renters property or personal liability policies.

"I don't want a Mail Boxes Etc. address in case that owner decides to close or relocate," she said. "The bottom line is that my home is where I conduct business. So my office becomes 'Suite 100' at my home address."

SOHO SNAPSHOT:
A TECHNOLOGY 'SAFETY BLANKET'

April Spring, president of Spring & Associates, an investor relations and corporate administration firm, works from an office on the second floor of her home. From there, she can survey her yard and the walkway to her home. This way, she can see when a knock at the door is a delivery person, a friend—or a stranger. Her neighbor knows that Spring works from home and has agreed to keep an eye on her.

Spring uses Caller ID to screen incoming calls and, as part of her "security blanket," keeps her Nextel cellular phone and two-way radio close at hand. With the touch of the radio's button, she's immediately connected with her husband Alex, or his 50-person group at Motorola.

Although the home has a back room ideal for an office, Spring opted for the peace of mind of the upstairs bedroom. "I felt so unsafe [in the backroom], like I was waiting for someone to come. I want to be in the front and up high so I can look down and see everything," she said. "I take security very seriously. Precautions give me peace of mind and allow me to concentrate on my work."

NOTES:

NOTES:

NOTES:

APPENDIX

NOTES:

INDEX

alarm systems, 10, 16, 23, 41-45
anti-virus software, 14, 19, 98-100
attachments, 85, 99

backup
    data, 17, 19, 107-109
    battery, 44, 51, 63, 95-97
business centers, 75, 76, 80

chairs/seating, 51, 53, 126, 128 129
childproofing, 55-57
confidentiality
    client protection, 79-83
computer locks, 120

deadbolts, 1, 3, 13, 16, 31-36

earthquake preparation, 60-63
electronic mail, 38, 85
emergency action plan, 18-20, 49
engraving, 121
ergonomics, 7, 13, 20, 124, 127-128,
espionage (prevention), 17, 83, 86
executive suites, 74, 75, 78

file cabinets (fireproof), 54
fire extinguisher, 1, 10, 13, 16, 59, 125, 139
firewalls, 100-104
first-aid kits, 125
foliage/plants, 1-3, 10, 13, 16, 23, 24-26, 133, 138, 140

hacking
    protection, 6, 19, 94, 98, 100-102, 106, 108
home invasion
    prevention, 17, 24, 75
hurricane preparation, 40, 60, 68
identity theft, 79-83, 87, 140
insurance
    computer, home, liability, personal, business owner's policy, 2, 10, 16-17, 19, 50, 64, 68, 70, 87-90, 118, 121, 127, 138, 140
inventory, 50, 52, 54, 64, 87, 120

laptop
    anti-theft, 6, 14, 61, 64, 84, 90, 94, 97, 108, 112-113 118-121, 123
lightning strikes
    protection, 90, 95-96

locks
    computer, 120
    doors, 1, 3, 13, 16, 31-36

mace, 1, 11, 15, 59, 139-140
meeting places
    alternatives, 77-79

natural disaster
    preparation plans & action plans, 14, 17, 18, 20, 60-63, 66, 87

INDEX

occupational safety & health administration, 7, 125-127
OSHA, 5-6, 125-126

personal audible alarms, 29, 118
plans
  safety plans, 18, 66-68, 118
plants/foliage,1-3, 10, 13, 16, 23, 24-26, 133, 138, 140

recycle bin, 84

safes
  locking storage devices, 52-54
security action plan 3, 11, 17-19
seating/chairs, 51, 53, 126, 128 129
stress management, 131-133
surge protectors, 95-96

telework centers, 73
telework/telecommute (–er, –ing), 1, 7, 12, 14, 20, 65, 66, 71, 73, 84, 90, 112, 124, 126, 141
telephone headsets, 126, 129
travel, 6, 11, 14, 17, 38, 65-66, 81 94, 108, 112-117

UPS
  (uninterrupted power supply), 95

vehicle safety, 112-114

window protection, 1-3, 11, 13, 15-16, 19, 23-24, 30, 34, 37, 38-41, 64, 138

ABOUT THE AUTHOR...

Jeff Zbar, the "ChiefHomeOfficer.com," has worked as a home-based journalist, author and small business advocate since the 1980s. In early 2001, he was named the *U.S. Small Business Administration's 2001 Small Business Journalist of the Year*.

As a writer, author, speaker and consultant, Jeff's specialties include work-at-home, teleworking, alternative officing and small business marketing, technology, security, communications and motivation. His think tank and consultancy, Goin' SOHO! (small or home office), works with corporations hoping to target the emerging home office and teleworking markets, and individuals hoping to enter or excel in the home-business, small business and teleworking arena.

Jeff writes for more than a dozen national publications, and is or has served as a contributing editor to *Home Office Computing*, *Entrepreneur's Home Office*, and *Writer's Digest*. He writes "Home Base," the teleworking advice column on Network World's Net.Worker Web site. He is the weekly marketing columnist and recurring small business feature writer for the *South Florida Sun-Sentinel*. His recurring columns also have been featured on Onvia.com (SOHO Corner Office) and FreeAgent.com (Go SOHO!).

Jeff's works include *Home Office Success Stories* (Goin' SOHO!, 1997), *Home Office Know-How* (Upstart, 1998), and *Your Profitable Home Business Made E-Z* (on CD-ROM, from Made E-Z Products

Inc., 2000), which was named the 2001 Editor's Choice Business Software Tool by ComputerTimes.com. He also is the author of the forthcoming book, *SOHO Psychology: Mastering the Mindset of Working from Home* (spring 2002). Jeff publishes *Home Office Success Stories*, a free monthly ezine on working from home and teleworking (www.goinsoho.com/successstory.cfm).

Jeff consults with corporations hoping to understand and target the home office worker and small business owner. His marketing and promotional efforts have included marketing message development and national speaking and/or satellite media tours for Office Depot Inc., BellSouth Inc., Sony Corp., HotOffice.com, and a successful fall 2000 national home office contest for Sprint Corporation.

Comfortable in front of the microphone, camera or a live audience, Jeff has extensive presentation and television experience. He has served as a recurring home office expert guest for WFOR/Channel 4, the CBS affiliate in the Miami-Fort Lauderdale market, and is a bi-weekly guest on Jim Blasingame's *Small Business Advocate* nationally syndicated radio show. Jeff frequently lectures for organizations serving the home office segment.

Jeff works and lives in suburban Fort Lauderdale with his wife and three young children.

Safe@Home: Seven Keys to Home Office Security…

… makes an excellent gift, informational / instructional resource, corporate incentive, product sales enhancement, and value-added merchandising and promotional tool for:

- Marketers of safety- & security-related products and services
- Retailers selling safety & security products
- Security-conscious companies with corporate telework programs
- Friends of home office workers

Books can be imprinted with company or product names on the cover button (which currently reads: "Hundreds of Tips for Entrepreneurs & Teleworkers"). Contact Jeff Zbar directly to discuss customized, bulk orders of *Safe@Home*.

Jeff Zbar also is a veteran lecturer, and is available for presentations, seminars, and keynote addresses on a wide range of small or home office (SOHO) issues, including safety & security, motivation, marketing, business strategy, organizational development, home office / small business psychology, and professional / personal balance issues.

For additional news, trends and information on small or home office (SOHO) safety news and topics, visit:

www.goinsoho.com/safe@home.html To contribute tips and ideas for future versions of *Safe@Home*, send your thoughts to **jeff@goinsoho.com**

Jeff Zbar's Goin' SOHO!
Toll Free: 888-467-6461
Home Office: 954-346-4393   Fax: 954-346-0251
Email: jeff@goinsoho.com   Web site: www.goinsoho.com
P.O. Box 8263 Coral Springs, FL 33075-8263